FACING the Future

LHBEC

Beyond the Earth Summit

Johan Holmberg, Koy Thomson and Lloyd Timberlake

Photographs by Mark Edwards

IIED

INTERNATIONAL
INSTITUTE FOR
ENVIRONMENT AND
DEVELOPMENT

EARTHSCAN

FACING the Future

Contents

Opposite page: The "million homes" programme in Sri Lanka helps poor families with low-interest, accessible loans.

Introduction

The United Nations Conference on Environment and Development (UNCED or the "Earth Summit") in Rio de Janeiro last June was the largest and most complex conference ever organised by the UN. It was attended by 178 governments, and there were some 120 Heads of State at the Summit that concluded the conference. The preparatory process had taken two and a half years and generated floods of words and reams of paper. The event had extensive press coverage. Debates on how to follow up the conference outcome are in progress all over the world.

This report summarises the main lessons from UNCED relevant for the work of those who, like ourselves, grapple with the environment and development agenda: governments, aid agencies, NGOs and academics. It is not simply an account of the conference as history. Rather it tries to explain how the Summit changed the face of the Environment/Development landscape and institutions, and it lists the targets and timetable agreed in Rio. Yet given the size and range of the conference documentation, any attempt to draw conclusions must be subjective and coloured by the perspective of the onlooker.

We have attempted to provide a guide for the reader who is interested in the issues involved but not necessarily well versed in all their details. The focus is on the conference outputs and their relevance. But we have also tried to describe the flavour of the negotiations leading to these outputs by pointing out principal controversies and stumbling blocks.

We start by providing our assessment of the outcome of the Earth Summit and go on to suggest some broad lessons to be learned from what was said (and left unsaid) in the UNCED documents. We list 12 of these, all of which we feel are of general, cross-cutting importance. The conference generated five formal documents: treaties on climate change and biodiversity, a statement on forest principles, the Rio Declaration and the action programme, *Agenda 21*. We comment on each of these by turn, highlighting major features as well as strong and weak points. There is a section on UNCED and its implications for the UN system, and we end with a fictitious dialogue on the conference outcome. Interspersed with this text are boxes on some issues of special importance. The appendices provide the full text of the Rio Declaration and the contents of *Agenda 21*.

The illustrations, and their captions, say something about the event and its setting: the conference itself at the spanking new Rio Centro, the NGO Global Forum some 40km away, the huge city of Rio de Janeiro with its opulence and extreme poverty, heavy security everywhere, along with masses of people and vehicles.

The report is a collaborative effort. Johan Holmberg supplied the initial concept, coordinated much of the work and wrote part of the text. Koy Thomson contributed sections and helped to edit the text. Mick Kelly and Sarah Granich wrote on the climate change convention, Steve Bass on the Forest Principles, and Lee Kimball on UN institutions. Simon Lyster provided valuable material on the biodiversity convention. Lloyd Timberlake lightly edited these various contributions. The pictures were taken by Mark Edwards and the report has been designed by David King. It has been written as part of the IIED 1992 programme financed by the governments of Denmark, Netherlands, Norway, Sweden and the UK, and we are obliged to them for their support.

Opposite page: Surui children watch a bulldozer carve an uncertain future, in the form of a logging road, through their Amazon forest reservation.

1: Was Rio a Success?

The outcome of a conference should be judged against its stated objectives. The mandate for the UN Conference on Environment and Development (UNCED), more popularly known as the Earth Summit, was established by the UN General Assembly resolution 44/228 of December 1989, a very wide-ranging document that raised an array of complex environment and development issues.

On many of these issues there is little scientific, let alone political, consensus: for example "the relationship between environmental degradation and the structure of the international economic environment". The resolution uses language that later came to haunt the negotiating process. For example, it talks about the need to identify "new and additional financial resources" for developing countries and also about transfer of "environmentally sound technologies" on "concessional and preferential terms" to these countries.

The resolution also calls for "specific agreements and commitments by Governments for defined activities to deal with major environmental issues", allowing for many different interpretations. It may be argued that the resolution establishing UNCED did not set a very workable mandate for the conference.

Later in the planning process, the UNCED Secretary-General, Maurice Strong, presented to the second Preparatory Committee (Prepcom 2) in March/April 1991 operational guidelines for the meeting. He listed the "potential outputs of the conference" as follows:
■ global conventions on certain issues (climate, biodiversity and possibly also forestry);
■ an "Earth Charter" as a basic declaration of principles to govern the relationships of people and nations with each other and with the Earth;
■ a programme of action called "*Agenda 21*" for the implementation of the principles of the Earth Charter;
■ new financial resources to underwrite *Agenda 21*;

■ a programme of technology transfer from rich to poor nations of "environmentally sound technologies";
■ strengthening the international institutional machinery, notably the UN, to carry out the foregoing.

It is easy to agree with Strong when at UNCED's closing session he expressed his disappointment with the political commitment shown by some of the 178 nations attending. In fact, the immediate conference result falls well short of his stated intentions. It represents the lowest common denominator of national interests, the inevitable effect of the UN insistence on consensus.

The treaty on climate change was weakened by US refusal to allow timetables and targets for reductions of greenhouse gas emissions. The biodiversity treaty was also weakened by the United States, which ended up not signing, largely because it felt that the treaty compromised its biotechnology industry. The statement on forest principles makes many useful points about forest management; but it is non-binding, and it is not clear what attention governments will pay to it.

The action programme, *Agenda 21*, covers almost every conceivable issue related to sustainable development. It contains many useful ideas. But if it is to be of practical use, the most important elements must be separated out and translated into operational plans at national and international level. It remains largely unfinanced, since the rich countries only agreed to meet a small fraction of the estimated cost of its recommendations.

The "Rio Declaration" was heavily

Opposite page: The Tree of Life, the symbolic heart of the Global Forum, which was the *non*-governmental heart of the UN Conference on Environment and Development in Rio.

compromised during negotiations. Rather than the punchy ten commandments-type statement originally envisaged for the Earth Charter, it became a bland declaration that provides something for everybody. The Commission on Sustainable Development, upon which UNCED agreed, is potentially one of the most important institutions established by the conference. It provides a mechanism whereby the World Bank and similar institutions, as well as national governments, can be held responsible for any failure to live up to the precepts of sustainable development.

Though these immediate results of UNCED fall short of stated intentions, it would be wrong, indeed arrogant, to judge this huge conference only in the light of its short-term achievements. It has been a momentous exercise in awareness-raising at the highest political level. No leading politician can any longer claim ignorance of environment and development linkages. It is therefore quite conceivable that future international debates on issues related to these issues will be more enlightened and move forward faster.

Indeed, it is difficult to escape the conclusion that the conference has set in motion some very large, if slow moving, wheels. Take the climate treaty: although it lacks binding targets, it does commit ratifying countries to controlling emissions and allows for stronger measures if necessary. Neither of the two treaties established in Rio is perfect, but they do launch long-term processes for dealing with two of the most pressing and complex global environmental concerns of the day.

Everything now depends on how the principles expressed in Rio, and the bargains struck between rich and poor countries, are put into force. Here the Commission on Sustainable Development may well prove to be useful in monitoring and improving the performance of governments and international institutions. In conclusion, it is far too early to pass judgement on UNCED. It will be several years before the verdict is at hand.

On the Meaning of Desertification

Of all the sectoral issues of environment and development, only one is explicitly referred to in UN General Assembly resolution 44/228, which paved the way for UNCED. That was desertification. No mention is made, for example, of deforestation, soil erosion, or marine pollution. UNCED had as its objective to "accord high priority to drought and desertification control ...".

It responded by including in chapter 12 of *Agenda 21* a decision that work is to be initiated towards an international convention on desertification. This was an initiative much promoted by the African states, which look to it as a vehicle to raise additional aid funds.

Desertification has long dominated much of the debate on environmental problems in Africa. However, despite much discussion, the meaning of the term "desertification" is less than clear. Many assumptions remain unchallenged, and many questions remain unanswered:

■ What is meant by "desertification" and "dryland degradation"? How can one measure it and assess its importance? Why is there such a fog of misunderstanding surrounding the term and the uses to which it is put?

■ What are the linkages between dryland degradation and climate change at either local or global levels?

■ Is there an "acceptable" level of degradation?

■ Are there useful policy tools which could help governments to improve resource management and use in dryland areas potentially vulnerable to degradation?

Recent research has shown that many of the processes held to be part of desertification have not been taking place. In dryland areas supposed to be subjected to advancing desert, there have been large variations in rainfall from year to year and consequent high variability in tree, grass and crop production. In the face of such climatic factors, the impact of human activities is insignificant.

Criticism of the muddled and inconsistent way in which the term has been used has led UNEP to revise its definition to cover the degradation of soil and vegetation within the arid, semi-arid and sub-humid zones caused largely by harmful human activities. This redefinition of desertification has been helpful in removing from consideration changes in resource productivity due to rainfall variability alone. It has also helped shift attention to areas where problems of resource degradation are most important.

Desertification, or dryland degradation, does not pose its greatest challenge on the desert edge, where few people live and where there is little productive activity. Rather, attention is needed in higher-rainfall zones where dense human and livestock populations put considerable pressure on available resources, and where inappropriate land use can bring about serious problems of soil erosion.

If problems of desertification are to find a sympathetic audience amongst donors, the issues need to be better defined. Only then can solutions be suggested. Very real and serious problems exist in many parts of dryland Africa. We might get closer to addressing them if we resolved to ban the term desertification once and for all.

Opposite page: The world's media cover the world's governments.

"US Singled Out as Eco Bad Guy"

This was the top headline of one of the conference newspapers during the Earth Summit. It rather aptly summarises the position that the US delegation found itself in as a result of the positions taken by the US administration not only in Rio but throughout the UNCED process.

The US did not sign the biodiversity treaty; it significantly weakened the climate treaty by refusing to agree to any specific targets or timetables; it did not hold out even vague promises for additional aid; and it single-mindedly argued for market-based solutions, even in the face of their potentially adverse environmental consequences. Some wondered whether the United States had a secret agenda to wreck the conference.

By adopting such positions, the United States was able to hold the entire conference hostage to its views. Throughout the UNCED process, the United States chose not to exercise leadership in the debates, but because of its size and power it still held an inherent veto over the outcome. The United States is the world's single largest economy, both in terms of consumption and pollution. It contributes about one-quarter of all emissions of CO_2, the main greenhouse gas. It generates more municipal waste than all other OECD (Northern) countries combined. It has a lead in many industrial processes, notably biotechnology, which rely on raw materials from natural resources in developing countries. With the United States as a disinterested player on the sidelines, efforts to grapple with the global environmental issues will without doubt be less effective.

The US participants in the debates had clearly thought through the issues involved; most of them were highly skilled and presented their case forcefully. The head of the US delegation in Rio and director of the US Environmental Protection Agency, William Reilly, clearly wanted a more flexible brief. But his hands were tied by the White House. There the legacy still prevailed of John Sununu, President Bush's former chief of staff, who had strong doubts about the link between greenhouse gases and climate. This translated into the position that protection of the environment would damage the US economy. "My only concern is US jobs", Bush said shortly before Rio. More specifically, there were worries that reductions of CO_2 emissions would upset US oil and coal producers. Surely, a major lesson to be derived from the Earth Summit by the UN is never again to hold a major international conference in a US election year.

As it was, the White House spelled out its positions poorly, even when it was arguing its own corner. It did propose a forest initiative and some money to support it, but this one constructive proposal only made the rest of the US UNCED record stand out in sharp contrast. Senator Al Gore, the Democratic candidate for Vice President who was in Rio, argued that the weakness of the forest principles, let alone any hope for a treaty on forests, was the direct result of the Bush administration's refusal to go along with any binding commitments in the climate treaty. "The handwriting has been on the wall ever since the climate change treaty was watered down", Gore said. "At that point it became inevitable that the G77 would resist putting all the focus on forests to absorb the carbon dioxide that is not going to be limited from the North".

At the end of the Summit, the US delegation released a note called "Interpretive Statements for the Record by the US" to highlight the US stance with regard to the Rio Declaration, *Agenda 21* and the Forest Principles. Here the United States disassociates itself from several of the statements in these documents. It made clear, for example, that "references to the sharing of benefits derived from the use of biological and genetic resources are understood to be without regard to the source of such resources", a major sticking point in the biodiversity treaty. It also stressed that the United States has never accepted the UN target of 0.7 per cent of GNP as aid and that, therefore, the United States "is one of the 'other developed countries' that agree to make their best efforts to increase their level of ODA", as stated in chapter 33 of *Agenda 21*.

There were reports that some Europeans secretly were grateful to the United States for its stance, which took the heat off all the industrial countries for burdensome greenhouse gas reduction commitments. The European countries could, some said, gratefully abandon their own proposals on the grounds that they would be worthless in the absence of US consent. Others argued that some EC member countries would not necessarily agree to enforce strict stipulations in a treaty anyway, as experience indicates that not all EC countries comply with what they agree to in Brussels. Whatever foundation there may have been for such speculation, the fact remained that the United States was very isolated in Rio.

The Business Council for Sustainable Development (BCSD) report, presented by 48 chief executives of major international corporations, was strangely at odds with President Bush's views, which he regarded as pro-business. US BCSD members met with Bush shortly before Rio and told him that it was precisely the companies and the nations which were *not* environmentally efficient and resource efficient which would soon lose competitiveness. They noted that Professor Michael Porter, at Harvard Business School, reported after a global study that it was the nations with the most rigorous environmental standards at home which often led in the export of the very products affected by those standards. Porter mentioned the success of Germany and Japan, and also the success of the chemicals, plastics and paints industries of the United States.

It will not be in the long-term interest of the United States to remain outside the biodiversity treaty. US firms will risk isolation in the future development and use of biotechnology. Since most transactions in this area, whether in developed or developing countries, are likely to proceed under the terms of the treaty, US companies may find themselves at a disadvantage. This may well prove more costly to the United States than any financial commitments under the treaty.

The stance of the US government on these issues will probably change. The US environment NGOs present in Rio were disgusted with the administration's position, and the NGO member of the official US delegation resigned in protest. They represent a powerful US opinion that Bush is likely to have underestimated. Sooner or later the United States will reclaim a role in the international debate on environment and development that is equal to its influence in other areas.

2: Twelve Lessons from the Earth Summit

A new phase in the North/South relationship

UNCED provided an important benchmark in the pattern of global relations of power and influence between nations and blocks of nations. Following the dissolution of the Soviet Union, the East/West confrontation is dead. The fault line has shifted 90 degrees from East/West to North/South, and bitter divisions of wealth and poverty marked many of the most acrimonious debates during the UNCED process.

UNCED also illustrated limitations to the US superpower status. The United States appears ill at ease and uncertain about its role in a North/South confrontation. On several issues it either chose not to exercise leadership or was unable to do so; on some other issues, like forestry, its movements were poorly timed and its position ineptly stated.

The new North/South relationship can somewhat paradoxically be characterised by increasing income differentials and by growing Southern influence. There is no question that the new world economic order is heavily slanted in favour of the North and that, as a result, economic disparities are widening. In 1976 the average income of countries classified by the World Bank as low – the poorest countries – was only 2.4 per cent of that of the high income countries; in 1982 this figure was 2.2 per cent, and in 1988 it had fallen to 1.9 per cent. This is the reality behind the strident calls from the South for rapid increases in transfers of financial and technical resources.

Current Northern consumption patterns are responsible for the emissions that are gradually poisoning the global environment and causing climate change, diminishing biodiversity and a receding ozone layer. But population growth and development needs in the Southern countries mean that, within a generation, their emissions may well surpass those of the North. These countries also command many natural resources, notably the tropical forests and their rich genetic heritage, that the North feels need to be managed in the global interest. Thus Southern governments will gradually gain influence and power in global environmental affairs, and will have an increasingly strong case for demanding access to the technology that would delay the rate of increase of their emissions. At the Earth Summit, the North was able to hold back on demands for increasing resource transfers to the South, and that debate was essentially resolved in the

North's favour. But in years to come, the North may be forced to be more accommodating.

If international debates are increasingly conducted along a North/South axis, it is also evident that the negotiating blocs are far from cohesive or internally coordinated. It is difficult to decide where to place the former Eastern bloc, which at times wanted to identify with the North, at others with the South. The Southern bloc, a spectrum stretching from Argentina and South Korea to Somalia and Zambia, often constituted a rather incongruous grouping, united only by an interest in getting as much aid as possible out of the North. Even the EC, supposedly the best coordinated group of nations, was unable to reach internal consensus on some important issues, such as financial resource transfers.

So the lesson is that we may in future years see more heated debate along the North/South divide, but often conducted in a disjointed fashion with special interest groups forming around specific issues, as they did in Rio. Environment and development will be fixtures on the future North/South agenda. This may be one of the main results of Rio.

Above: A bank guard in Mexico City. She is effective against armed robbers, but less effective against bankers and diplomats. Little was done in Rio to stem the debt-induced outflow of wealth from countries like Mexico.

Foreign aid: it is not only size that matters

The single biggest disappointment for the developing countries was the failure of UNCED to generate significantly increased aid flows. This is amply reflected in some of the post-conference commentary by G77 member countries[1]. The issue on financial resources dogged the preparatory process from early on, when it became apparent that the requisite financial resources to pay for *Agenda 21* would not be at hand. The final conference outcome on this particular score was even weaker than scaled down expectations only weeks before Rio. In the event, only some US$2.5 billion in additional aid was pledged (exact numbers are difficult to compile), to be compared to the estimated cost of *Agenda 21* of US$125 billion in additional annual flows, and to Strong's late hopes of US$10 billion.

The OECD countries were not about to give in on this issue, even if it meant placing in jeopardy the conference outcome. There is some truth in the statement made by President Bush on the eve of his departure for Rio that "the time of the open cheque-book is over". The prevailing political doctrine in many of the rich countries with its focus on tax cuts and retrenchment of public services is not conducive to increased aid. The economic recession, the capital requirements of Eastern Europe, restructuring of the European Community, and electoral uncertainties in the US and elsewhere, all reduce the likelihood of any precipitous increases in foreign aid at this time.

Much of the debate was on the UN target of 0.7 per cent of donor country GNP to be given as foreign aid. Countries that already exceed this target waxed eloquent about the need for meeting it, while others refused. The EC was split on the issue with major countries such as France and Germany arguing for the target, the UK against it (with US consent). In the end, chapter 33 of *Agenda 21* only says that countries "agree to augment their aid programmes in order to reach that target as soon as possible".

Negotiations on this point were hard and protracted. No stone was left unturned, no argument went untested. The rich countries eventually prevailed, as they must: at the end of the day they cannot be made to give away resources against their will. The present stalemate, with Southern countries demanding more financial resources, and Northern countries refusing to provide them, may be expected to continue for some time to come.

We would conclude from this debate that the attempt by the conference secretariat to raise huge additional financial flows, probably against better judgment and with an eye toward the wishes of the G77 countries, represents outdated thinking that harks back to the 1970s. Aid flows do not have the importance attributed to them to make the world more sustainable. At least equally important are issues like sound economic and social policies, good governance, proper economic incentives, and an effective regulatory framework. None of this is new in the aid vocabulary. But all of it will need more emphasis in the years to come.

The recent turmoil in European currency markets and the resultant fiscal austerity packages in some donor countries will further reduce the likelihood of any increases over the next few years in foreign aid. In fact the signs are of substantial cuts in aid budgets from almost all donors. This was clear at the IDA-10 pledging conference in Washington in September 1992, where the outcome fell well short of pre-Rio expectations, and at meetings of the OECD's Development Assistance Committee held at about the same time.

Nevertheless, increased aid will remain important in a number of areas such as health and education services, infrastructure and research. With aid flows falling well short of demand, this raises a host of issues relating to how existing flows are deployed. This in turn recalls old aid issues, such as targeting aid better on the most needy, the extent of tied aid, and the use of aid for large capital-intensive projects versus small labour-intensive ones. It will be important to get away from the excessive focus on the size of aid budgets, almost the sole aspect of aid discussed at UNCED, and instead concentrate increasingly on the *quality* of aid. It certainly is not only size that matters.

No discussion about North/South financial flows can be complete without a reference to two related issues that were barely mentioned during the conference proceedings, although *Agenda 21* has brief references to them: debt and foreign

Top: The London Stock Exchange. Capital markets must be reformed so as to support rather than destroy the livelihoods and environments of farmers – such as these in Chattera village, India (above).

trade. Both have potentially important implications for Southern countries to sustainably finance their own development, yet both go begging for solutions that allow them to serve this purpose. The outcome of the GATT talks and more widespread application of Trinidad-terms for debt reduction will therefore have important implications also for the result of UNCED[2].

In summary, then, it will in future years be as important as ever to carefully husband foreign aid resources, target them better, and provide them with fewer strings attached. Some aid donors try to have it both ways: they argue against large quantitative increases, while at the same time eroding existing aid programmes from within by tying procurement and giving priority to large, capital intensive projects. Quality of aid should be at the forefront of discussions, even if aid quantity remains difficult to increase.

1 The G77 group represented the developing countries throughout the UNCED process. In 1991 it was led by Ghana, in 1992 and in Rio by Pakistan
2 GATT is the General Agreement on Tariffs and Trade, the ongoing process to negotiate reductions in international trade barriers. Trinidad-terms is a formula for providing debt relief for the poorest heavily indebted countries undergoing economic structural adjustment.

The need to harness market forces for sustainable development

The prevailing economic policy paradigm emphasises "free market" mechanisms over government command-and-control interventions. This model is apparent in a variety of contexts, national and international, and is much in evidence in current debate. It has guided the creation and increasing integration of the European Common Market. It is guiding the GATT attempts to eliminate trade barriers. It underlies the ongoing trends in many countries to privatise public services. It has been given added impetus by the failure of socialist economic systems to generate growth and development.

Reliance on market forces goes hand-in-hand with deregulation, a trend equally evident in countries as different as the United Kingdom and Uganda. Big government is thoroughly discredited in both industrial and developing countries, partially as a consequence of the demise of the socialist model and its reliance on central planning. Government bureaucracy is to be reduced, parastatal companies privatised, public services at least partially put on a commercial footing, and government intervention in the market minimised. Chapter 2 of *Agenda 21* exhorts governments to "remove the barriers to progress caused by bureaucratic inefficiencies, administrative strains, unnecessary controls and the neglect of market conditions" and to "encourage the private sector and foster entrepreneurship". This mind-set, very different from the models of 20 years ago, underlies much of the UNCED documentation.

The logic of this reasoning with regard to the environment is that economic growth is seen as a *sine qua non* for sustainable development. Unleashing market forces is essential for growth. No growth means more poverty, which degrades the environment, whereas economic growth will generate the resources that allow the environment to be protected, reduce poverty, provide resources for growing populations, and even decrease population growth.

But there is no evidence at all to suggest that market forces by themselves protect the environment. There is, on the other hand, plenty of evidence that unfettered market forces can quickly degrade the environment. Fuelled by the lure of short-term economic gain, these forces are powerful. The issue, then, is how to get the best out of market forces – economic growth, and the efficiency and innovation which often accompany competition – while bending the forces toward environmental protection and equity of opportunity. Put differently, the question is how to determine the appropriate level and type of regulation by government.

Like the quality of foreign aid, this is an old debate that needs to be revisited in the light of UNCED. In developed countries with strong institutional frameworks, it is mostly a question of fine-tuning existing instruments. But for developing countries with weak institutions, it entails a laborious process of capacity-building, during which ongoing processes of degradation, fuelled by market forces, still do damage. It raises issues related to governance: the need for better policy formulation, improved planning and management of environment-related matters in development, and strengthened legal and institutional frameworks. Many of these issues are well covered by Chapter 8 of *Agenda 21*.

This is an area of considerable importance, underlying the prospects for effective action in many other areas. *Agenda 21* makes a strong case, in Chapter 8 and elsewhere, for "environmentally sound pricing" of products and services. In the context of aid there will be a need for donors to develop programmes under the rubric of "governance for sustainable development" and to coordinate their initiatives in that regard. What is needed is not costly in terms of scarce foreign aid; little hardware and few major investments are necessary. But it does require quality commitment by donors to initiate action, sometimes in areas where their own expertise may be limited, such as "integrated environmental and economic accounting", a programme area in Chapter 8.

Above: Unemployed youth in Britain. The rich – poor divide exists within as well as between countries.
Top: Middle class home in Sri Lanka.

action plans on the global level. Yet it is on the national level that the precepts of *Agenda 21* can be made meaningful and operational. This is where there is knowledge, concern, involvement and the capacity to act. Only more concerted action at that level can solve the global environmental problems.

This is recognised in the Preamble to *Agenda 21* and continues as a cross-cutting theme in many chapters. Chapter 8 calls on each government to "adopt a national strategy for sustainable development". Chapter 37, National Mechanisms, says that all countries should be "building a national consensus and formulating capacity-building strategies for implementing *Agenda 21*". Chapter 38, International Institutional Arrangements, states that "national-level efforts should be undertaken by all countries in an integrated manner so that both environment and development concerns can be dealt with in a coherent manner". The chapter goes on to say that the aid agencies "should make greater efforts to integrate environmental considerations and related development objectives in

their development assistance strategies" in order to "better support national efforts to integrate environment and development".

There are already a variety of approaches to integrating environment and development in national plans. In his statement to the conference the President of the World Bank promised that the bank would do this in all its borrowing countries. The World Conservation Union has a widely applied approach to what it calls "strategies for sustainability". Various bilateral donors have their own methodologies. A likely outcome of UNCED

The imperative of national strategies for sustainability

UNCED tended to focus on the global issues, and *Agenda 21* is an aggregation of

The role for foreign aid in this context is clear. More needs to be done to develop participatory methodologies for sustainability strategies. It is necessary to emphasise process over product and to take the long view, since such strategies may well take years to complete. Many developing countries will require support in areas like human resource development, institution-building, and policy dialogue, the "quality" type assistance mentioned above. But they will not be helped by efforts by well-meaning donors to do the work for them. National strategies for sustainability will be one of the necessary conditions for *Agenda 21* implementation.

It is a major opportunity for future work, a chance to tackle in a coherent fashion conflicting development objectives. It is important that it is done properly.

The need for capacity-building in developing countries

Capacity-building in developing countries is one of the major themes running through Section IV, "Means of Implementation", of *Agenda 21*. It is discussed in the contexts of technology transfer (Chapter 34), science for sustainable development (Chapter 35), education, public awareness and training (Chapter 36) and national strategies for sustainability (Chapter 37). Clearly, this is seen as a major focal area for international cooperation in years to come.

Chapter 34 suggests that capacity-building in the context of technology transfers can be achieved through, *inter alia*:

■ human resource development;
■ strengthening of institutional capacities for research and development, and programme implementation;
■ integrated sector assessments of technology needs, in accordance with national plans for *Agenda 21* implementation.

Transfer of technology was one of the key issues at UNCED. It was also one of the most controversial, with the entire text relating to this subject bracketed (not agreed) after the preparatory meetings. Contentious issues included terms of technology transfer, intellectual property rights, and transfer of privately owned technologies, but these were all resolved in Rio.

A study commissioned by the United Kingdom on the role of technology transfer in combating climate change suggests that most of the "environmentally sound" technologies required are already available to developing countries . Access to them is more a perceived problem than a real one, the study says. With the right price signals, commercial companies will be motivated to obtain and successfully absorb new technologies. But a sustained effort will be required to facilitate absorption, and this requires more attention to "soft" technologies, such as

Above: Training in soil conservation in the Cameroons.
Left: A cycle rickshaw takes children to their school in Delhi.
Top: A visit by the local family planning officer in Sri Lanka.

will be a much enhanced effort to carry out national sustainability plans in poor, and perhaps also in rich, countries.

But, as recognised in Chapter 37, such plans will only be effective if they evolve gradually as a result of a participatory process that engages different social groups in open debate on the merits of the various trade-offs involved in reconciling environment and development objectives. Bringing in a group of high-powered foreign consultants to produce an investment plan will likely result in a blue-print that is not "owned" by the government involved, so the government

will feel little commitment to it. The recent history of development is full of efforts wasted on such plans.

Preparation of national plans for sustainable development will test the democratic governance of developing countries. A government that is not responsive to its citizens, and that is authoritarian, corrupt and remote, is unlikely to be able to produce strategies to deal effectively with environment and development concerns. For such a government, protection of the environment will usually yield to short-term considerations of economic growth.

Above: Migrants set up houses beside a Mexico City railroad, where older children care for their next generation.

training, management and maintenance. This is an important area for capacity-building with support through foreign aid.

Chapter 37 establishes two specific objectives in the context of national sustainable development strategies:

■ by 1994, each country should complete a review of its capacity-building requirements for devising such strategies;
■ by 1997, the UN Secretary-General should submit to the General Assembly a report on the strengthening of technical cooperation programmes for sustainable development.

These two targets should ensure that national strategies, capacity-building for sustainable development, and aid for these purposes will remain focal areas for international cooperation in the years to come.

Conventions on the environment: more to come

UNCED confirmed that the environment is fast becoming the third pillar, together with security and economic issues, of the emerging international system of the 1990s and beyond. Two resultant developments are currently under way.

The first is that these three areas are becoming increasingly interwoven and difficult to keep apart. As it is becoming more widely accepted that the environment is a scarce resource to be better protected and husbanded, there is increasing likelihood that the environment will be the cause of conflicts, and may be used as a weapon in hostilities, as Iraq did during the war in Kuwait.

Secondly, there is a proliferation of international institutions related to the environment, as this area catches up in

prominence with security and economic issues. There are several hundred multilateral and bilateral environmental conventions, most of which have been signed during the last decade. The report of the Business Council for Sustainable Development (BCSD) said that international environment problems should be solved by treaties rather than, as is often the case now, by unilateral trade restrictions. So we are likely to have many more institutions in years to come. Environmental diplomacy is surely a growth area.

The two conventions that were signed in Rio are both legally binding for ratifying nations. They are both weak treaties, due in part to the position adopted by the United States. The call in the climate convention for industrial nations to stabilise greenhouse gas emissions at 1990 levels by 2000 is not legally binding. There is nothing in the text on biodiversity that compels countries to protect their biodiversity. However, the conferences of parties to the conventions may well amend them later to add substance, and provide financial resources in support of implementation. A precedent is the rather toothless Vienna convention from 1985 on the ozone layer that was given muscle (money) with the Montreal protocol from 1987.

The industrial nations set out wanting a binding forest convention, but the G77 group put paid to their hopes. The opposition of developing countries centred on national sovereignty. They viewed their forests as part of their natural resource endowment to be exploited as they saw fit. They made it clear that they would be prepared to set aside part of that endowment, provided that they were compensated for lost revenue. In other words, they would be willing to sign away part of that sovereignty at a price to be paid in increased aid. Since more aid was not forthcoming, no treaty was possible.

Chapter 12 in *Agenda 21* on desertification contains a recommendation

to begin the process to prepare a convention on desertification, "particularly in Africa". This was a sop to the African countries, which argued as a group for this convention, mainly as a vehicle to raise more aid. Despite the fact that the UN Environment Programme (UNEP) has already tried and failed to address the issue, and scholars argue that the very definition of desertification is problematic (see Box 1), the UN General Assembly in autumn 1992 set in train a two-year process to negotiate a Desertification Convention. The African countries might do better by convening a donors' conference to address *all* their difficult development problems, of which desertification is but one.

Another convention recommended by Chapter 17 deals with oceans. It suggested convening a UN conference to identify and assess problems related to the conservation and management of highly mobile fish stocks, and to consider international cooperation on fisheries, consistent with the Law of the Sea convention. This approach appears more promising. Some argue that the oceans will rapidly become more important in the debates over carbon sinks and biodiversity, rather like the tropical forests have been in the 1980s, and that knowledge of their role is far too incomplete.

UN institutions: some winners, some losers

The World Bank emerged as a clear winner among international organisations. The donors had no time for the proposal of the G77 for a Green Fund, nor for the notion of a separate fund attached to each convention. Despite objections from G77 about the Bank's lack of democratic governance, there is essentially no other financial mechanism available that inspires the confidence of the donors. The Global Environment Facility (GEF) which the Bank administers (jointly with the UN Development Programme (UNDP) and the UN Environment Programme (UNEP), although their roles are more modest) will be roughly doubled in size, and substantial additional resources had been provisionally pledged to the International Development Association (IDA) for use in the poorest countries.

The precise amounts were to be established after the tenth funding replenishment conference of IDA (IDA-10) in the autumn of 1992 (as this was being written). But set against a global recession and declining aid budgets, the prospects for substantial increases seem poor. IDA is now the single most important source of concessional funding for developing countries. The ninth funding replenishment (IDA-9) was set at US$15.5 billion. To adjust for expansion of the world economy and inflation, IDA-10 would have to be increased by about US$2 billion. There was much discussion in Rio about a possible increase to IDA beyond the correction in real terms that would raise it by US$5 billion, otherwise known as the "Earth Increment". Of this money, US$1.5 billion would come from World Bank interest income and the remaining US$3.5 billion from industrial country donors. In the event, it proved impossible to reach agreement on explicit text on this issue.

References in *Agenda 21* to other UN agencies are rather more equivocal. Chapter 38 stresses that UNDP has "a crucial role" in the follow-up to UNCED but it avoids the key issues of how UNDP's mandate could be strengthened, or how it could be provided with additional resources. UNEP should equally be "enhanced and strengthened" to undertake new roles such as providing technical and policy advice to governments, but there is no activity by governments to provide extra resources for such commitments. The UN Conference on Trade and Development (UNCTAD) receives such a tepid mention that it must be questioned whether it now has any role at all, as most initiatives on trade are taken in the context of GATT.

There is talk in Chapter 38 about the need for regional and subregional cooperation, but there is surprisingly little emphasis on the regional development banks, the only regional institutions with significant resources. The sectoral chapters of *Agenda 21* dutifully make mention of the UN specialist agencies concerned. However, the profile of the UN agencies overall in the UNCED documentation is low, even when it might have been expected not to be. For example, FAO, the Food and Agriculture Organisation, is indisputably the UN agency responsible for forestry, but it was never suggested that it play an active role in the work on the forest management principles, apparently because it is distrusted by rich and poor countries alike. There is little in the UNCED documentation to contradict the thesis that UN system reform is long overdue.

The Commission on Sustainable Development was established by the conference as a body to oversee the integration of environment and development by the UN system and progress towards implementation of *Agenda 21*. It will have 52 country members from all continents and report to the UN General Assembly through its Economic and Social Council (ECOSOC). After long debate it was agreed that it would monitor the performance of not only international organisations, such as UN agencies and the international banks, but also of governments. Chapter 33 on financial resources states that the commission "would regularly review and monitor progress (by governments) towards the target" (of 0.7 per cent of GNP for aid). Details were worked out by the General Assembly in autumn 1992. If governments are prepared to make effective use of this new body, and there are some signs that they will, it could become a valuable and long-needed

watchdog on the progress towards sustainable development objectives. If so, this would be a major accomplishment.

Business and industry: the beginning of a trend?

The Earth Summit was not only the first time that over 100 heads of state have sat down to discuss common issues. It was also the first occasion that business and industry have played an important and constructive role in the run-up to a global

Centre: At the foot of Rocinha, army tanks shield Earth Summit delegates from the inhabitants above.
Above: Official delegates arriving at Rio Centro.
Top: Children at home in Rocinha, Rio's largest slum.

UN conference, if not so much at the conference itself.

UNCED Secretary-General Strong had appointed Swiss industrialist Stephan Schmidheiny to be his principal adviser on business and industry. Schmidheiny invited key chief executive officers from five continents to join his Business Council for Sustainable Development (BCSD). Some of the better-known of the 48 companies represented – by officers representing themselves rather than their companies – include ABB, Ceiba-Geigy, Chevron, Du Pont, Mitsubishi, Nippon Steel, Nisson, Shell, 3M and Volkswagen.

By the beginning of Rio, the Council had produced a 350-page report, commercially published in six languages as a book entitled *Changing Course: a Global Business Perspective on Development and the Environment*. The Council held a meeting in Rio and a press conference before the Summit began proper (as did the much larger International Chamber of Commerce, ICC). The Council supported "free markets" and "market forces", but argued that capitalism could not survive if those markets did not reflect environmental as well as economic truth. They called for stricter enforcement of the polluter pays principle, and for prices which reflect environmental costs. They urged governments to consider greater use of "economic instruments", such as environmental taxes and saleable pollution permits, rather than command-and-control regulations.

Another main message was that there are a number of trends working in the world which will encourage businesses toward economical and environmental excellence. Those firms which are not "eco-efficient" - able to maximise added value while minimising resource use and pollution – are essentially unviable and will not remain competitive for long.

This message was psychologically very powerful and also contradicted President Bush's expressed fears that environmentalism would make firms *less* competitive. So the Council's views were picked up in most of the world's major newspapers. Schmidheiny and his staff then spent the first week of the Summit doing what other NGOs were doing – lobbying to have their positions accepted. They spoke at Global Forum presentations, lunched with World Bank leaders, breakfasted with US senators, and spoke to outside gatherings, such as the Junior Chamber of Commerce and a group of "spiritual and parliamentary leaders".

This exercise was very successful in terms of attention and column inches, but of course it is much harder to judge its effect upon the Summit. Chapter 30 of *Agenda 21* deals in a rather vague and summary fashion with business and industry. With that exception, there were few UNCED documents which affected business directly, while the Council's conclusions tended to be addressed more to individual businesses and to individual governments.

In his address to the Earth Summit plenary, Schmidheiny called for new partnerships between governments and business to work particularly on such issues as technology cooperation, new economic instruments, and establishing "enabling conditions" for investment in developing countries. Indeed, the long-term result of the presence in Rio of the Council, and also of the ICC, may be a growing willingness by business to participate in such gatherings, and also a growing willingness by governments to accept and encourage that participation. Rio may thus have witnessed the beginning of a trend.

Meagre pickings for the poorest countries

The poorest countries had looked to the Earth Summit for a confirmation of their development needs and the aid resources to address those needs. They were bitterly disappointed. Although *Agenda 21* and other conference documentation says much about what should be done to foster development, little aid money was pledged in support. On the contrary, UNCED resolutions stress the role of institutions such as the World Bank and GATT, which the poorest countries see as undemocratic and bureaucratically opaque.

One particular group that arguably was shortchanged more than others was the countries of sub-Saharan Africa. Their combined product is less than that of Belgium. Their recent history has been marred by a combination of political upheavals, economic mismanagement, and repeated droughts. In some countries, such as Somalia, Zaire, Mozambique and Liberia, the authority of modern government has all but ended, and development has been set back by decades. Other countries, such as Kenya and Malawi, may have fared better economically but seem set for future disruptions due to repressive governments. Overall, living standards are no better in Africa today than they were at the time of independence in the 1960s. There is no group of countries more in need of sustainable development.

Yet these countries seemed singularly unable to articulate a common position and to argue their case at UNCED. There was no African caucus that made any noticeable impression and there were few coherent African positions on the major issues. By contrast, the small island states, infinitely less visible than the Africans, were able to lobby successfully for a special section in *Agenda 21* (chapter 17 on oceans has a programme of action called "Sustainable development of small islands").

The complex UNCED negotiating process was taxing on poor countries with small delegations unable to monitor several concurrent debates. But there was little evidence of any concerted effort by these countries to organise representation

in the different working groups. Only rarely was an African position on an issue clearly spelled out, and for the most part the Africans hid behind the larger G77 group.

In the end, the Africans won their argument for an international conference on desertification to be convened by 1994, a weak platform from which UNEP has tried unsuccessfully to raise more aid resources. Their case for more aid would have been better served by an explicit recognition on their part of the need for more transparent and democratic governance and for an economic and social policy framework conducive to sustainable development. By taking the lead in this debate, they could conceivably have defused arguments of donors wishing to link policy conditionality to aid flows. As it was, one lesson which emerged from the Earth Summit is that the poorest countries, and the Africans in particular, need to organise themselves better in order to hold their own in protracted and complex international negotiating processes of this kind.

Participatory development: the key to sustainability

The Earth Summit, with all its heads of state, top civil servants, and diplomats, can be seen as very much a traditional top-down international talking shop. But it did manage to generate much language supportive of a participatory, bottom-up style of development, one that is favoured by voluntary groups and grassroots organisations. In fact, NGO lobbying lies behind much of this text.

Examples abound throughout *Agenda 21*. Chapter 3 on combating poverty states

Above: Alcoa reforestation of bauxite mines in Australia.
Top: Sustainable plywood production in Bhutan.
Opposite page, top: Women collecting fuelwood in Burkina Faso.
Bottom: Niger herders and their animals.

that "governments... should support a community-driven approach to sustainability" that would "establish new community-based mechanisms and strengthen existing mechanisms to enable communities to gain sustained access to resources needed by the poor to overcome their poverty". Chapter 5 on population calls for "an effective consultative process" to ensure that the views of women and men are well reflected in the design and implementation of programmes.

Chapter 6 on health talks about the need to "establish mechanisms for sustained community involvement in environmental health activities". Chapter 7, Human Settlements, calls on cities to "institutionalise a participatory approach to sustainable urban development, based on a continuous dialogue between the actors involved in urban development". Similar statements are found, for example, in chapter 11 on forests, chapter 12 on desertification and chapter 14 on agriculture and rural development.

There are also chapters in *Agenda 21* that give explicit support to so-called "major groups", such as women, children and youth, indigenous people, workers and trade unions, and NGOs. All of these chapters stress the need for active involvement by these groups in order to make sustainable the environment and development programmes that affect them. Here there are clearly several lessons to be noted by governments and aid agencies.

The women's groups were particularly successful in spelling out their requirements. Their representative, Bella Abzug, was the only speaker at the concluding plenary debate to receive spontaneous applause during her speech.

What is less clear is whether governments have taken on board what participation actually means in practice. For example, chapter 10 on land resources includes a call to "encourage the principle of delegating policy-making to the lowest level of public authority consistent with effective action and a locally driven approach". Chapter 14 on agriculture and rural development has activities to "assign clear titles, rights and responsibilities for land and for individuals or communities to encourage investment in land resources" and to "develop guidelines for decentralisation policies for rural development through reorganisation and strengthening of rural institutions".

Such issues are often fraught with complexities in developing countries, and governments' failure to attend to them often explains the failure of rural development programmes.

So while UNCED has provided a strong endorsement of the need for participatory approaches to sustainable development at community level, the steps needed to bring this about in many countries will remain subject to dispute. Again, progress will hinge on the availability of equitable policies and public institutions attuned to participation by the most needy.

People get organised: **Above:** Brazilian Indians at the Earth Summit.
Centre: Traditional tribal "environmental" dance, Cameroon.
Top: Signing by thumbprint for agricultural loans in India.

UN conference methodology: the need for more product and less process

It is difficult to believe that governments will ever allow an agenda as complex as that of UNCED to come before them again. The truism that everything is related to everything else is not a basis for good decisions and operational work. It creates a context rather like a great trade fair in which everyone is selling, but few are buying.

On the substantive issues, particularly on finance, there was little concerted effort by delegations to bridge the North/South divide. Governments seemed only to be listening to each other in order to fix the texts, not to change their positions. With a more tightly-drawn agenda there could have been movement; but with so many issues under consideration concurrently, all delegations could do was to negotiate what was essentially the status quo.

The complexity of the agenda, and of the issues involved, created a tendency to focus on the negotiating process itself rather than on its final product. There was endless talk about scheduling new meetings, much less about concrete targets and timetables. At times it seemed as if the expected outcomes of the exercise, the agreements and commitments by governments, had been all but forgotten.

There is reason for disappointment with regard to the hard and fast commitments made in Rio. But part of this disappointment arises out of the raised expectations, generated not least by the hype emanating from the conference secretariat itself (such as Strong's repeated statements that this was "the most important meeting in the history of mankind"). The raised expectations were part of the momentum generated by the sheer size of the whole exercise.

In Rio, Norwegian Prime Minister Gro Harlem Brundtland courageously questioned one of the UN holy grails, the consensus rule. The strength of this working method is that it can afterwards be claimed that everybody was on board. But the weakness is that as a consensus is patched up, countries with strong and deviant views may allow themselves to be swayed by some clever manipulation of text while nothing of substance has changed. This tends to reinforce the emphasis on process over product in the proceedings.

For example, one of the most intractable issues late in the conference was the refusal by Saudi Arabia and Kuwait to agree to chapter 9, protection of the atmosphere, on the grounds that it placed an over-emphasis on energy efficiency and conservation, a naked display of self-interest by some of the wealthiest countries on the planet. While adjustments to the text eventually allowed agreement on the chapter, Saudi Arabia formally placed on record its reservations at the final plenary to underline that nothing, in its view, had really changed. It is then relevant to ask what purpose is served, at the end of the day, by the consensus rule.

There are several lessons that can be learned from the way in which this massive exercise was conducted. These include the need for a simpler agenda, less hype and raised expectations, less emphasis on the negotiating process itself and more on its expected outcome, and an examination of the implications of removing the consensus rule.

NGOs – a forward push

What does a woman dressed as a cow, a billionaire aboard a yacht, and a member of staff of IIED have in common? It is not the billions. In Rio, they were all classified by the Earth Summit organisers as members of non-governmental organisations. This example well illustrates the difficulty of conveying what NGOs are, and what they do. The one generalisation which can be made is a negative one: they are not government. NGOs include business groups, trade unions, local government, scientists' groups, the traditional non-profit peoples' organisations and even the International Federation of Police Officers.

The billionaire, by the way, is a founding member of the Business Council for Sustainable Development, and the cow a member of a group campaigning for vegetarianism.

The fact is that, in UN terms, NGOs have had an unprecedented opportunity to participate in and influence the preparation of the Earth Summit, but less chance to participate in the event itself.

Some of the toughest inter-governmental fights at the first preparatory meeting concerned the rights of NGOs to speak and make written submissions to the official plenary. NGOs won this right, but of course were barred from actual negotiation. NGOs were also granted discretionary rights to attend "informal" meetings. Many NGOs were official members of government delegations, with access to classified briefs and closed negotiation sessions. Some actually found themselves in the awkward position of negotiating and speaking for their governments. Others were close advisers to the conference secretariat. Many groups organised in their own countries to produce national sustainable development reports which were far better than those of their governments.

Was it worthwhile? In terms of influencing the actual texts, undoubtedly. Whole chunks of *Agenda 21* can be traced to NGO drafting groups and coalitions. One example is the section in the poverty chapter on "empowerment", which completely changed the orientation of the text. Women's organisations were the trail-blazers of a theme which runs

Rio's conscience: Above: Children weave through the Global Forum.
Centre: Japanese campaigners for Minamata victims.
Top: Environmental organizations taking to the air.

throughout *Agenda 21*: citizens' participation in decision making, with a particular emphasis on the role of women. Another theme, that of taking actions and making decisions as close as possible to the people, was pushed by NGOs. The Commission on Sustainable Development was given a significant boost by NGO lobbying. Many other examples can be found, and we should not forget that the fact that the Earth Summit was happening at all was due, in some measure, to the persuasive skills of environment and development organisations.

Chapter 27 in *Agenda 21* deals exclusively with NGOs, even establishing the somewhat fatuous objective that by

1995 "a mutually productive dialogue" should have been established between all governments and NGOs on sustainable development. The chapter calls on both UN agencies and governments to be more receptive to, and supportive of, NGOs. In addition, chapter 38 on international institutional arrangements underlines the role of NGOs in the UNCED follow-up process. Given the initial resistance (notably from some G77 countries) to a wide NGO participation in the UNCED process, NGOs could hardly have hoped for a more propitious outcome.

With all this success, why weren't NGOs in Rio elated and heralding the Earth Summit as a triumph? The general mood had definitely changed from that of the Prepcom meetings, which seemed open and welcoming of participation.

For one thing, the NGO scene had become far more complex, and its focal point, the Global Forum, had by the Brazilian government's design (for security and other reasons) become severed from the official Earth Summit which had been placed far out of town at the Rio Centro centre.

NGOs were divided in Rio. There were the lobbyists and activists with official accreditation (1,420 accredited, with 2,400 individual passes into Rio Centro), who worked the official meetings and fed the appetites of the media with quotes and stunts. There were many thousands of other NGO representatives, from advocates of breast-feeding and hashish, to sober policy analysts enjoying the togetherness of the Global Forum but not much concerned with, or oblivious to, Rio Centro. There were those NGOs who had long given up on the official Earth Summit, and were either involved in negotiating alternative treaties designed to strengthen common NGO agendas and ways of working, or in exchanging grassroots experience at the Earth Parliament. There were other NGO groupings doing their own quiet but effective lobbying in many meetings around town.

But compared to the Prepcoms, governments clammed up in Rio. In the view of many NGOs, government briefs were tight and unyielding, with instructions to give away as little as possible, and to turn action wherever possible into process. Physical separation between the government event and the NGO event, the extraordinary richness and diversity of NGOs which made a common voice almost impossible, and the realpolitik of governments, all worked against bold, new or innovative initiatives.

Time and original expectations will be the judge of whether or not Rio was a success. Rio delivered no instant solutions but many opportunities. The overall conclusion must be that for NGOs concerned with environment and development, Rio represented a push forward, a raised profile, and an added recognition by governments and international organisations. The issue now will be how to move forward from there.

3: The Biodiversity Treaty

Developing countries now demand a greater share of the economic benefits arising from the use of resources within their boundaries. Until now, these benefits have mainly accrued to the industrial countries with the technological capability to exploit them. At the same time, the developed world has become increasingly apprehensive about the accelerating rate of loss of biodiversity and its global consequences such as the effects of tropical deforestation upon global climate change for example.

These parallel concerns led to the negotiations for a treaty on biological diversity, starting with a draft prepared in 1987 by IUCN. Formal negotiations commenced in November 1990 under the sponsorship of UNEP. They were concluded in Rio when 153 nations, excluding the United States, signed the treaty to protect biological diversity and to use it sustainably. Negotiations, conducted in parallel with the UNCED Preparatory Committee meetings, had been arduous and often acrimonious, with heated arguments mostly along the North/South divide.

Throughout, the treaty is consistent with *Agenda 21*, which covers both biodiversity (chapter 15) and biotechnology (chapter 16).

Highlights of the treaty

The preamble contains many important principles, including innovations such as recognising "the vital role that women play in the conservation of biological diversity" and the "desirability of sharing equitably benefits arising from the use of traditional knowledge, innovations and practices (of indigenous and local communities)". Reflecting the concern of many countries, especially developing ones, that the treaty should not give the international community any rights over the management of a nation's biological resources, the preamble affirms that conservation of biodiversity is a common concern of all mankind, and that states are responsible for using the biological resources sustainably, but that states have sovereign rights over their own biological resources.

The overall objective of the treaty is the conservation of biological diversity, sustainable use of its components, and fair and equitable sharing of benefits from the use of genetic resources. The latter is to be achieved through "appropriate" access to genetic resources, "appropriate" transfer of relevant technologies and "appropriate" funding (Article 1). In addressing technology and sustainable use, this treaty goes far beyond existing, narrowly defined conservation conventions, but some feel that it has done so at the expense of a more rigorous treatment of specific actions on global biological diversity.

Each party ratifying the treaty is required to develop national strategies, plans or programmes for the conservation and sustainable use of biological diversity, or adapt existing plans to this purpose. Another requirement ("as far as possible and as appropriate") is the integration of conservation and sustainable use of biodiversity into relevant cross-sectoral plans and policies (Article 6).

Under Article 7, each party is required (as far as possible and as appropriate) to identify important components of biodiversity, and monitor them, particularly those parts requiring urgent conservation action, or which offer the greatest potential for sustainable use. Article 7 also requires the identification and monitoring of those activities which have or are likely to have significant adverse impacts on the conservation and sustainable use of biological diversity.

Conservation *in-situ* (that is, in the wild) is deemed to be the fundamental principle for the conservation of biological diversity, with off-site measures such as seed banks having an important but less fundamental role to play (preamble). Each party is required to "establish a system of protected areas or areas where special measures need to be taken to conserve biological diversity". Further, biological resources important for biodiversity conservation should be regulated or managed, whether inside or outside protected areas, to ensure their conservation and sustainable use (Article 8). This is important since it could be used to argue that the exploitation of, for example, fish stocks and forests must be regulated and be made sustainable. It is interpreted by some as potentially the first legal underpinning for sustainable management of all natural resources.

Conservation *ex-situ* shall be supported "predominantly for the purpose of complementing *in-situ* measures" and facilities shall be established, "preferably in the country of origin", to help recovery and reintroduction of threatened species. Financial support for the establishment of such facilities in developing countries is encouraged (Article 9).

Each party was bound to integrate conservation and sustainable use of biological resources into national decision-making, protect and encourage customary use of biological resources in accordance with traditional cultural practices, support local populations in this regard, and encourage cooperation with the private sector in the sustainable use of biological resources. However, all of this is qualified by the phrase "as far as possible and as appropriate" (Article 10).

Article 11 requires each party to adopt "economically and socially sound measures that act as incentives for the conservation and sustainable use" of biological resources, again "as far as possible and as appropriate". In the context of the GATT, and at a national level, the issue of agricultural subsidies is clearly relevant.

The treaty obliges each party to facilitate access to genetic resources for environmentally sound uses, although access must be "on mutually agreed terms" and "subject to prior informed consent", so there is some discretion. Parties are encouraged to conduct their research on genetic resources, "where possible", in the country of origin. They should share benefits arising from commercial use of genetic resources with the party providing the resources (Article 15). This provision was the source of some of the strongest US objections to the treaty. It means, for example, that a pharmaceutical company producing a drug based on genetic material from a developing country should not only carry out its research in that country but also share the eventual profits resulting from sale of the drug.

Parties also undertook "to provide and/or facilitate" access to and transfer of technologies (including biotechnology) of two types:
– those that are relevant to the conservation and sustainable use of biological diversity, and
– those that make use of genetic resources and do not cause significant damage to the environment.

Opposite page: Threatened swamp in Thailand, home to vulnerable forest species of plants and animals.

Access to and transfer of these technologies is to be provided and/or facilitated for developing countries "under fair and most favourable terms, including on concessional and preferential terms where mutually agreed". Where the technology is subject to patents and other intellectual property rights, the treaty specifically states that the transfer should be consistent with the protection of intellectual property rights (Article 16).

Article 19 provides for the participation in biotechnological research by parties, especially developing countries, who provide the genetic material. It also enables them to enjoy "priority access on a fair and equitable basis" to results and benefits arising from research. The need for a protocol on the safe transfer and use of living modified organisms (the treaty's euphemism for genetically modified organisms, which the US objected to any mention of) resulting from biotechnology, will be considered.

Each party agreed to provide financial support "in accordance with its capabilities" for national measures to achieve the treaty's objective. Developed country parties "shall provide new and additional financial resources to enable developing country parties to meet the agreed full incremental costs" of implementing the treaty. Developing country obligations to conserve biological diversity are made dependent on "the effective implementation" by developed countries of their commitments relating to finance and transfer of technology. Developing country conservation obligations will also "take fully into account the fact that economic and social development and eradication of poverty are the first and overriding priorities" of the developing countries (Article 20).

A mechanism was agreed for the provision of financial resources to developing countries for purposes of the treaty. This mechanism shall function under the authority and guidance of the Conference of the Parties, that is, the group of nations ratifying the treaty (Article 21), to be convened by UNEP not later than one year after the treaty comes into force (Article 23). Article 21 nearly caused Japan and the UK not to sign the convention. Their worry (and the worry of 17 other nations who signed a declaration to the effect), was that Article 21 would be interpreted to mean that the Conference of the Parties – the majority of whom are developing countries – would have the power to decide the financial contribution of the donor countries. However, Article 23 makes clear that decisions on rules of procedures are made by consensus. A secretariat will be established (Article 24) which Switzerland and Spain have offered to host. The treaty also established a committee to provide the Conference of Parties with scientific, technical and technological advice (Article 25).

The treaty will enter into force 90 days after it has been ratified by 30 countries (Article 36), and it can be amended by the Conference of Parties (Article 29). In Rio, 153 countries signed the convention. Wry observers put the large number of signatories down to the US not signing.

Criticisms from the Southern NGOs

Vandana Shiva wrote in the Third World Network's magazine *Third World Resurgence* that "the Biodiversity Convention started out primarily as an initiative of the North to "globalise" the control, management and ownership of biological diversity... so as to ensure free access to the biological resources which are needed as raw material for the biotechnology industry". She went on to offer a number of criticisms of the treaty from a Third World people's perspective:

– The convention "is too strong on patents and too weak on the intellectual and ecological rights of indigenous peoples and local communities".
– The convention is built on the "assumption that biotechnology is essential for the conservation and sustainable use of biological diversity". According to Shiva, biotechnology substitutes for biodiversity, treating it merely as a "means of production", and results in the replacement of diversity in agricultural and other systems with uniformity.
– The convention has accepted patents in the area of living resources.
– The convention has excluded the world's crop gene banks, many of which are based in the developed world. Since the convention did nothing to clarify ownership of seeds held in Northern gene banks and collected in the South, and since the convention deals only with access to genetic resources to be collected in the future, the fear is that industrial country governments will patent the genes held in these banks. Developing countries would have to pay for any biotechnological products arising from these seed banks despite the fact that the genes originated in their countries.

US opposition to international biosafety regulations meant that the technically accurate term "genetically modified organism", was replaced by a new term "living modified organism resulting from biotechnology". But despite US objections, Article 19 requires consideration of the need for a protocol on biotechnology and safety issues. *Agenda 21* on the same issue simply calls for guidelines. In the view of developing world activists, protection of biodiversity depends upon protection of the peoples who have been custodians of biodiversity throughout the ages. They see the United States as simply protecting business interests, through patent regulation to protect industry profits, and opposition to international safety regulations which might have threatened profits.

How effective is the treaty?

Replying in advance to criticism of the treaty as too vague, weak and watered down, Dr. Mostafa Tolba, the Executive Director of UNEP, said after the final text had been agreed in Nairobi in May 1992:

"With this treaty we have established the minimum on which the international community can agree. I know there are those, particularly among NGOs, who are scornful of such bare minimums and who argue that the world will not be saved by them. They believe that no agreement is better than a weak one. I disagree with this line of reasoning, although I respect the sincerity of those who profess it. I think that the process of international environmental law requires us, for better or for worse, to walk before we run and to crawl before we walk."

He went on to point out that concluding the treaty was the essential first step in a process that with time could lead to more forceful commitments, including the provision of adequate financial resources.

His statement summarises rather well the status and perceived role of the treaty. It establishes new legal commitments on conservation, finance, access, technology transfer and benefit sharing that are likely to make it an important instrument for the conservation of biological diversity in the years ahead. It has both conservation and development objectives, and there is a strong link between the needs of people and conservation.

However, it is largely a "framework" agreement, setting out principles which will need elaboration by future meetings of the Conference of the Parties before they can be expected to be fully effective. The wording of the treaty is rather weak with many obligations being qualified by "as far as possible" or "as appropriate". The provisions on intellectual property rights and transfer of technology are confusing, and there is little on important policy and institutional issues such as land reform, empowerment of communities, and incentives to biodiversity.

Among the most contentious issues in the treaty are its financial aspects, including the nature of the funding (voluntary or UN assessed contributions) and the choice of an institution to handle it. It was decided to leave the nature of countries' contributions to the first Conference of the Parties. Animated debate led to the decision to have the Global Environment Facility (GEF) handle contributions on an interim basis until treaty signatories decide upon a permanent arrangement.

Opposite page, top: High-tech tree cloning in Western Australia. Bottom: Low-tech tree nursery in Sri Lanka.

4: The Convention on Climate Change

One hundred years after the Swedish scientist Arrhenius warned that coal-burning might change the climate, it is time to take stock. The world has warmed by 0.5°C, and we now have a Framework Convention on Climate Change. But will this treaty help or hinder humanity's response to the fundamental threat of global warming?

The intensely political process of drafting the convention has resulted in a text not so much characterised by compromise but by an effort to avoid the resolution of conflicting positions through vagueness and ambiguity.

The preamble to the convention acknowledges that human activities are enhancing the natural greenhouse effect which will result in an additional warming of the Earth's surface, which "may adversely affect natural ecosystems and humankind".

It states that "the largest share of historical and current global emissions of greenhouse gases has originated in industrial countries, that per capita emissions in developing countries are still relatively low and that the share of global emissions originating in developing countries will grow to meet their social and development needs".

Although recognising scientific uncertainties and the need to continuously re-evaluate actions on the basis of new findings, the preamble also recognises that "various actions to address climate change can be justified economically in their own right and can also help in solving other environmental problems". In other words, many actions taken to cope with climate change are what policy makers call "win-win" actions. The need for industrial countries to take immediate action is recognised, as are the special difficulties of countries dependent upon fossil fuel production, use and export, and the vulnerability of island states and countries with sensitive ecosystems.

The stated objective of the convention is the "stabilisation of greenhouse gas concentrations... at a level which would prevent dangerous anthropogenic interference with the climate system". This should be achieved "within a time frame sufficient to allow ecosystems to adapt naturally..., to ensure that food production is not threatened and to enable economic development to proceed in a sustainable manner".

Setting aside the fact that humanity may already have changed climate beyond the bounds at which "dangerous interference" is inevitable, the vagueness of this objective creates ample opportunity for endless negotiation on subsequent protocols.

As any scientist could have informed the negotiators, defining a level of climate change within which ecosystem adaptation can occur naturally is virtually impossible. Food production is already threatened by climate change in many parts of the world. But who is to decide whether this is the result of natural or anthropogenic processes? Whose economic development should be allowed to proceed in a sustainable manner? And how will "sustainable" be defined?

Stabilisation of greenhouse gas concentrations in the atmosphere is a truly long-term objective. Governments usually talk of stabilising emissions. But some scientists have estimated that at least a 60 per cent reduction in emissions will be required to stabilise atmospheric concentrations of carbon dioxide, for example. Although no concentration is specified, this is an important principle. However, the convention is far from a binding undertaking actually to stabilise concentrations.

Article 3, the Principles, reinforces many of the points stated in the preamble, and indeed in the whole of *Agenda 21*, the Earth Charter, and the Biodiversity Convention. It is stated that protection of the climate system is for the benefit of present and future generations, and should be carried out in an equitable manner by industrial and developing countries, according to historic responsibility, state of development and capacity to respond.

The precautionary principle is recognised, along with the need to take into account cost-effectiveness, and "ensure global benefits at the lowest possible cost". A globally comprehensive approach is accepted as a principle, which means that cooperative arrangements can be reached between interested parties (joint implementation). So a rich country looking for the most cost-effective strategy for their share of emission reduction might pay a poor country to plant trees or clean up dirty industries, and take the credit for the resulting reduction.

Perhaps the most important text lies in Article 4, Commitments, and Article 12 "Communication of information related to implementation".

Opposite page: Steam and invisible gases belch from a Dutch steel mill.

Article 4 deals with control targets, and it is on this issue that the Convention on Climate Change is at its most confusing and convoluted. The only apparent indication of an explicit target for the industrial world is in Article 4, Commitments, which at one point refers to the "aim of returning (greenhouse gas emissions) individually or jointly to their 1990 levels". An earlier paragraph says that "return by the end of the present decade to earlier levels of anthropogenic emissions" will "demonstrate that developed nations are taking the lead in modifying longer-term trends... consistent with the objective of the Convention". Taken together, some commentators say that this is indistinguishable from a binding commitment to stabilise greenhouse gases at 1990 levels by the year 2000. Others, notably the United States, would firmly disagree.

The wording of the latter reference to stabilisation is perhaps more significant as an implicit recognition of the power of the position many Southern nations have taken on climate change: limited involvement unless those industrial nations with historical responsibility for the problem take action first. Is the primary motivation for stabilisation on the part of the industrial world concern for the planetary environment or a less than altruistic fear that rising emissions in developing nations may exacerbate the problem in decades to come?

In fact, stabilisation of emissions may not prove a particularly convincing or helpful achievement. Firstly, the slow economic growth expected in many industrial nations to the end of the century will stabilise emissions automatically. Secondly, even if the OECD nations meet this target, the rate of warming to 2100 will only be reduced by 5 per cent or so. Stabilisation thus represents little more than a commitment to "business as usual".

Article 4 reveals that the only firm commitment is that industrial countries should report on progress towards stabilisation – not that they should necessarily achieve this end. But the commitment to reporting is nonetheless strong and significant. Parties shall "develop, periodically update, publish and make available to the Conference of the Parties, in accordance with Article 12, national inventories of anthropogenic emissions by sources and removals by sinks of all greenhouse gases...". Parties shall "formulate, implement, publish, and regularly update" national and regional programmes to deal with climate change.

Left: Victims of flooding in Bangladesh. A man carries his cholera-stricken wife to a field hospital for treatment. Centre: Hurricane Andrew by satellite. Global warming has been blamed for such extreme weather conditions. Bottom: Raising the height of sea defences in Germany. Worldwide, 20 million dollars a year may have to be spent in building sea walls against the effects of global warming.

HURRICANE "ANDREW"

 Satellite: METEOSAT   Acquired: 24th August 1992

Image Format: TIVH   Time: 21:02 GMT   SPACE SECTOR

Article 12 describes the reporting obligations in more detail. After six months, to allow the convention to enter into force, industrial countries will have to submit an initial communication detailing inventories, control programmes and emission projections. Developing countries will report three years after they receive funding to cover both the full incremental costs of carrying out national reports, and the costs of taking action. Least developed countries will report at their discretion.

The adequacy of the approach described in Article 4 will be reviewed by the Conference of the Parties at its first session, with the possibility of amendment if necessary.

Although the United States may have achieved their objective in avoiding what they see as a binding commitment, they lost on the issue of wanting cuts in chlorofluorocarbon (CFC) emissions to be counted towards any reduction objective. Article 4 makes it clear that the convention relates to carbon dioxide and other greenhouse gases not controlled by the Montreal Protocol on CFCs.

Article 5 contains commitments to support, develop, and strengthen scientific research and systematic observation, and to improve developing countries' own capacity to carry out such research. The next Article concerns the need to promote the development and implementation of public awareness, education, and participation programmes in addressing climate change and its effects, and the training of scientific, technical and managerial personnel.

Article 7 establishes the work of the Conference of the Parties, which is the convention's supreme body, responsible for regularly reviewing implementation, developing comparable methodologies for greenhouse gas inventories, and general coordination and information exchange.

Articles 8, 9 and 10 establish a Secretariat, a scientific and technological advisory body, and an advisory body on implementation. The scientific and technological advisory body will assess the

latest scientific findings on climate change and the impact of the convention, and identify relevant technologies and advise on transfer. The implementation body will review national reports and assess the cumulative effectiveness of national actions on ameliorating climate change.

A mechanism for providing financial resources on a grant or concessional basis, for activities such as technology transfer is defined but not specifically identified under Article 11. As with the Montreal Protocol, the financial mechanism is the key to the convention, since the convention contains few, if any, specific obligations for developing countries. It is made clear in the convention that implementing commitments depends on money and technology transfer. Developing countries' participation will become increasingly important as their contribution to total global greenhouse gases increases. Unless the developing countries are drawn into taking action at an early stage through effective funding mechanisms, there is little hope of getting them to accept any future amendments binding them to action.

Under Article 4, the industrial countries (minus the Eastern European states), agree to meet the full costs of developing countries preparing national reports. They also agree to provide the financial resources for carrying out inventories, preparing adaptation responses, and preparing and implementing programmes to mitigate against climate change. The latter point could include conservation and enhancement of reservoirs and sinks, among other measures. The details of the funding mechanism (including the amounts of funding required, and a review of those amounts), are left to the Conference of the Parties but in the interim, the funding will go through the Global Environment Facility (GEF), after it has been appropriately restructured to ensure equitable and balanced representation and a transparent system of governance. To sum up, pending the reform of the GEF and the meeting of the

Conference of the Parties, there is no money on the table.

The remaining Articles, 13 to 26, deal with the legal aspects of the convention common to other treaties, such as amendments, resolution of disputes, entry into force, and ratification.

A separate resolution on interim arrangements requests the Secretary General of the United Nations to make the necessary arrangements for preparing for the first meeting of the Conference of the Parties. The first Preparatory meeting may not take place before the end of 1992.

Many of the criticisms of the convention were related to its weakness in terms of lack of binding commitments and firm targets. In fact, the main mechanism to make countries abide by the convention will not necessarily be legalistic, but may depend upon public accountability, openess, peer review, and pressure. Permanent and comprehensive reporting and review mechanisms substitute for clearly defined reduction targets in achieving the difficult overall objective of "stabilisation of greenhouse gas concentrations... at a level which would prevent dangerous anthropogenic interference with the climate system". This should be achieved "within a time frame sufficient to allow ecosystems to adapt naturally..., to ensure that food production is not threatened and to enable economic development to proceed in a sustainable manner". If this approach does not work, then the possibility for amendment and additional protocols is contained within the convention.

For most of the world's people, however, it is not controlling greenhouse gas emissions that is the priority, but ensuring adequate protection from the impact of climate change and sea level rise. Even with drastic cuts in emissions, some global warming is thought to be inevitable. This point was made many times during the negotiations, particularly by developing country delegates. That the convention does not mention the importance of facilitating human

adaptation is a lamentable deficiency.

On a more positive note, the historical responsibility of the industrial nations in creating the problem is acknowledged, as is the extreme vulnerability of the developing world. The treaty recognises the challenge faced by developing nations in ensuring that their socioeconomic development does not increase their contribution to global warming to an unacceptable level. Moreover, the convention clearly endorses the need for precautionary action regardless of remaining scientific uncertainties.

But the overwhelming impression is of a document based largely on the self-interest of the powerful, sprinkled with a few concessions to ensure the compliance of the rest.

There is no evidence that the world's politicians have understood the true import of climate change and its implications for the development process. And that is the main problem with the Framework Convention on Climate Change. Even a statement of principle alone, with no firm commitments, would have been preferable if it recognised the full significance of global warming and provided a clear agenda for action. As it is, we are left with an ambiguous document which will allow politicians to fiddle on as the world warms.

So, has the effort expended on developing the climate treaty been worthwhile? Whatever its limitations, the Framework Convention does clearly signal that the world's politicians are noticing global warming – whether as a result of genuine concern, defensiveness or fear. And, however cynical one might be about the many phrases inserted into the treaty to meet the demands of special interest groups, the underlying social, economic and geopolitical issues that climate change exposes have been aired and a forum created in which some resolution may ultimately prove possible.

The climate treaty represents a tentative first step; whether it is a step in the right direction remains to be seen.

5: Forest Principles

Forest issues were among the most contentious in Rio, with arguments polarised mainly along a North/South divide. During the Prepcoms, much of the North, notably Canada, Sweden, the United States, and the United Kingdom, had argued that forests, although situated in national territories, are of global importance, principally for their biodiversity and climate regulation functions. These countries argued that a degree of supra-national control of forests is desirable and therefore proposed a legally binding convention on forests.

The South, forcefully led by Malaysia and India with the support of the entire group of developing countries (G77), stressed the sovereign right of countries to use their forests for their development, through the actions of the various public, private and community groups in each nation. They argued that global notions of sustainability could not encompass these varied and legitimate needs, but that rather more effective national and local control of forests was needed.

The developing countries recognised that forests do provide global benefits. But they emphasised that, if there were to be a convention (an idea that most of them were set against), this would have sovereignty implications. Therefore, a compensation mechanism such as foreign aid would be essential to cover the revenue foregone by countries setting aside forest reserves to serve the global interest. When it was clear that no compensation mechanism would be forthcoming, all vestiges of support for a convention disappeared in the South. Many Southern diplomats charged that the North was seeking a forest convention as the cheapest way of cutting carbon emissions.

A problem that dogged the negotiations on forests was that work remained limited to the Prepcoms, with no parallel process available. Developing countries refused to set up additional meetings outside the framework of the Prepcoms, citing lack of resources. Besides, there seemed to be a general reluctance by all parties to use the Food and Agriculture Organisation, the UN agency responsible for forestry, as a facilitator.

The Forest Principles as a political process and document

By the time of Prepcom 4, governments realised that there was little scope, and no time, to negotiate any form of legally binding forest agreement. Besides, they were still divided over the need for one. Rather that wasting energy in a final clash over a possible convention, most sought a way to achieve a positive consensus on forests.

The result is the Forest Principles – the "Non-legally binding authoritative statement of principles for a global consensus on the management, conservation and sustainable development of all types of forests". These principles do, indeed, "reflect a first global consensus on forests". One of the most significant aspects of the Principles is that they recognise the usefulness of a universally agreed statement on forest management. No government walked out of the negotiations, although not all agreed with every paragraph. This might suggest both a recognition of the global importance of forests and a willingness to recognise demands that do not necessarily meet with national desires.

The Forest Principles is mainly a political document. It is in few senses an operational tool, and it should not be read as such. None the less, there are many levers within it for positive action.

In Rio, with only days left of the protracted UNCED process, the US made a public statement expressing support for a convention on forests and pledging financial backing. Coming, as it did, very late in a process in which the US had mostly played an unhelpful role, and with several key points left unclear (for example, whether the financial resources mentioned were truly "new and additional" or simply a reallocation within the existing US aid programme), it was seen as disingenuous and even cynical. It did not affect the course set for the Forest Principles.

What the Forest Principles say

The Principles cover all forest types and a wide range of associated environment and development issues. The "guiding objective of the Principles is to contribute to the management, conservation and sustainable development of forests, and to provide for their multiple and complementary functions and uses" (preamble). The importance of local forest peoples and of women is recognised, as is the need to support the economic interests of these groups in forest use.

The Principles note the need for valuing forests, setting associated standards, monitoring them, using environmental impact assessments (EIA) for forest developments, setting aside protected forests, developing plantations, strengthening national and international institutions, and also public participation. They meet generally accepted requirements, but they are not very specific as political statements, and they provide no institutional prescriptions. Thus, in an operational sense, they take us no further towards forest conservation and sustainable development.

The Principles should be read alongside chapter 11 of *Agenda 21*, "Combating Deforestation", and are consistent with the contents therein.

A brief analysis

The Forest Principles are not, of course, legally binding. But it is significant that "in committing themselves to the prompt implementation of these Principles, countries also decide to keep them under assessment for their adequacy with regard to further international cooperation on forests" (preamble). This would also seem to keep the door open for a future legally binding instrument, thus indicating that a principal Northern interest has not been entirely quashed.

The document also clearly puts over the Southern view. It is riddled with references to the need for additional financing and statements emphasising the importance of sovereign use of forests (Principles 1,2,8 and 9). However, the conclusion may reasonably be drawn that by having both reached a "first global consensus on forests" and by evoking sovereignty, nations have accepted responsibility for forests.

The challenge now will be to encourage countries to take up this responsibility, through the development of national responses to the Forest Principles. These responses should be harmonised internationally where appropriate, for instance, in respect of multilateral trade, biodiversity conservation and climate change – all global issues. Foreign aid has been the traditional mechanism for encouraging such responses, but a wider range of international agreements is also appropriate, especially in view of apparent restrictions on aid volume: trade, investment, technology cooperation, international monitoring of how the Principles are applied in practice, and (perhaps eventually and for certain issues only) international law.

Opposite page top: Carefully managed agroforestry in Bali.
Bottom: Forest burned to expand ranching in the Amazon.
Centre and right: Liming lakes and monitoring acid rain in Sweden.

6: The Rio Declaration on Environment and Development

The Rio Declaration (see Appendix 2 for full text) started life as the Earth Charter. Maurice Strong wanted a declaration that would be a short, uplifting, inspirational, and timeless expression of a bold new global ethic.

At an early point in the Earth Charter negotiations, the US delegation echoed this view, imagining the Earth Charter hanging in every child's bedroom, only to be sharply put down by a reminder from a developing country delegate that not every child had a bedroom. This incident epitomised the tension within the Earth Charter. Under the guidance of delegates who felt anything but uplifted and inspired, it became a distillation of many of the conflicts and political differences which infused the whole of the conference agenda.

In Nairobi at the first Prepcom session, delegates were told that the Earth Charter was to contain "the basic principles for the conduct of nations and peoples with respect to environment and development to ensure the future viability and integrity of the Earth as a hospitable home for human and other forms of life".

At the second Prepcom session held in Geneva, Strong laid out his ideas for the Earth Charter's relation to *Agenda 21*; "*Agenda 21* is envisaged as a programme of action for the implementation of the principles enunciated in the Earth Charter". The UNCED Secretariat produced a preliminary check-list of elements which might be considered for the Earth Charter, drawn from existing documents. At this point it became clear to delegates that the Earth Charter had no clear direction, and was more or less a free-for-all.

The final shape of the Earth Charter was largely determined during the third Prepcom session in Geneva, although it took firm control from the Chairman in Prepcom 4 to force through a Chair's draft when negotiations became gridlocked.

Initially, discussions developed from a consolidated draft which included 145 proposals grouped into 17 headings. Early on, the Malaysians expressed concern that "Earth" Charter was too environmental and that the name and emphasis of the document should be changed to reflect development concerns. Their suggestion was to call it the Rio Declaration on Environment And Development.

Lacking a strong central theme, the Charter slowly became a distillation of the political and conceptual arguments dogging the North versus South debate. This became the theme. Far from a timeless ethic, it was now a snapshot of history. There was no possibility for the Charter to become a serious consideration of the ethical and moral implications of sustainable development, which might at some stage be developed into legally binding conventions.

Inevitably, the consolidated draft got bogged down. As is practice in the UN, the largest consensus bloc, in this case the G77 countries, submitted their own Rio Declaration for consideration. This included statements on the sovereign right of nations to exploit their own resources, the right to development, the right of individuals to have freedom from hunger, poverty, and disease, and the responsibility of the richer countries to shoulder the greater burden of taking action on global environmental problems since they caused the problem in the first place. Throughout the preparatory process, the Declaration slowly evolved through a cycle of G77 texts, amendments, and Chairman's texts.

While the G77 countries emphasised development and global equity concerns, the industrial world emphasised issues centreing on governance and the environment.

For example, key elements of the United States draft included: the suggestion that the Declaration should be a prologue to *Agenda 21* and not a separately agreed document; respect for human rights and democracy; open and free markets, but that markets should reflect full economic accounting of environmental costs and benefits; and the polluter pays principle. The Scandinavian governments added concepts of environmental security; indigenous peoples and women; access to information, administrative and judicial procedures; and full internalisation of environmental costs. The European Community suggestions included greater clarity on burden sharing; linkage of unsustainable patterns of consumption and production with population policies supportive of sustainable development; environmental impact assessment; compensation for damage; participation and freedom of information; and environmental security. The Canadians put forward proposals for the resolution of environmental disputes.

The Declaration was all but completed in the fourth Prepcom session in New York, and despite fears that it would be re-opened during the Earth Summit due to an Arab/Israeli conflict over Principle 23, the text was finally accepted in Rio.

An important postscript to the Rio Declaration was the release by the United States delegation of "Interpretive Statements for the Record by the United States". These were in fact disclaimers on Principles 3, 7, 12, and 23. For Principle 3, the United States claimed that "Development is not a right... on the contrary, development is a goal we all hold". For Principle 7, they reject any interpretation which implies acceptance of any international obligations or liabilities. For Principle 12 they assert that under certain circumstances trade measures can be used to protect the environment, and for Principle 23, in plain English, the understanding of the United States is that the principle implies nothing. A cynical view is that the US would simply not sign on to the Rio Declaration if it implied any legislative or policy change whatsoever. The interpretive statements somewhat support this view.

A Commentary on the Final Rio Declaration

Principle 1 puts human beings at the centre of concerns for sustainable development, and contains a watered-down version of a right to a clean environment. Although the principle is fine as an emphasis on human development priorities, some feel that a serious sustainable development ethic should recognise the intrinsic value of the natural world, irrespective of its value to human beings.

The issue of sovereignty in Principle 2 restates a real and recurrent UN concern. Few commented on the irony that a summit devoted to shared global responsibilities, cooperation and partnership should so strongly assert sovereignty. A better formulation might have been to put sovereignty within the context of what is now known as the principle of subsidiarity (taking actions at the lowest most appropriate level).

The right to development described in Principle 3 is an important principle for the developing countries. Throughout the Earth Summit, developing countries pressed for an assurance that their basic development needs will not be compromised by the overdevelopment of the industrialised countries. For example, the fact that the richer countries have polluted the atmosphere to the extent that it threatens major climatic changes does not mean that developing countries must automatically stop developing. Most see the right to development as rhetorical

Above: A Buddhist monk brings an ethical and spiritual dimension to the Earth Summit.

rather than legal.

Following the non-contentious Principle 4 concerning the integration of environment and development, Principle 5 restates the UN commitment to cooperate to eradicate poverty, but makes two further important points: first, eradicating poverty is an indispensable requirement for sustainable development; and second, that sustainable development entails strong considerations of equity.

Debate on Principle 6 concerning the special needs of developing countries highlighted basic differences in North/South perceptions. Developed nations argued that this principle was out of place in the declaration since it involved the specific issues of finance and technology transfer which were addressed elsewhere in *Agenda 21*. The developing countries disagreed, saying that these were principles which cut to the heart of UNCED, and formed the very foundation of the new global partnership.

Principle 7 contains the principle of common but differentiated responsibility. This principle means that although all nations have a responsibility to develop in an environmentally sustainable way, a

greater responsibility lies with the developed nations. This is because historically the developed nations produced most of the pollution causing climate change and other global environmental problems. Also, because they are rich and have the technology, developed nations have a moral responsibility to help those developing nations which do not. Wording which suggested that there should be particular emphasis on the need for the richer countries to address their unsustainable patterns of consumption was toned down. The United States delegation said repeatedly that it rejects any interpretation of this principle which implies that they accept US obligations or liabilities.

The issue of population was to be tackled in Principle 8. However, since the mention of population is taken as being synonymous with blaming the South, population is always couched in terms of demographic policies, and always balanced with the parallel responsibility of the richer countries to eliminate overconsumption.

The active participation of well-informed and concerned citizens in the pursuit of sustainable development was a strong theme throughout *Agenda 21*. Principle 10 underscores this, with a principle which addresses the need for freedom of environmental information and effective access to judicial and administrative proceedings, including redress and remedy. This is an example of a principle which requires effective legal follow-up at a national level.

Principles 11, 12, and 14 address the interrelated issues of national environmental standards, trade, and the movement of dirty goods and industries.

The industry lobby had pushed hard for the harmonisation of environmental standards. Principle 11, however, addressed the concerns of developing countries that higher environmental and social standards would impose an unwarranted economic cost. Principle 11 therefore argues for country-specific

standards. This still leaves open the question of dirty industry moving to poorer countries with lower standards. But Principle 14, which calls on states to cooperate to ensure that there is no relocation of harmful activities and substances, may offset this.

A sizeable group of developing countries wanted an outright ban on the transboundary movement of toxic waste and other harmful substances. Principle 14 stops short of that, seeking only to cooperate to discourage or prevent relocation and transfer.

Principle 12, on international economy, trade, and environment, is a development principle which calls for a supportive and open international economy. It states that environmental considerations should not be used as disguised trade restrictions. In some respects this links to Principle 11. It does not answer the question of whether a country with high environmental standards for a product would be justified in imposing tariffs or even excluding products from countries with lower standards. *Agenda 21* discusses, without resolution, this same issue in greater detail.

Taken together, Principles 11, 12, and 14 present an ambiguous and in some part contradictory verdict on the desirability of free and unfettered international markets.

The controversial issue of liability and compensation for the victims of pollution and other environmental damage is covered in Principle 13. This principle urges the further development of law in this area. Although it goes no further than existing commitments, some in industry fear that the tougher absolute or retrospective liability which may result from Principle 13 may put them out of business.

Principles 15 and 16 are interpretations of the precautionary principle and a statement of the need to internalise environmental costs. Many feel that the precautionary principle is weakened by two qualifiers. The first is that nations should enact the precautionary principle "according to their capabilities", which gives plenty of opportunity to opt out. The second is the qualifier that actions based on the precautionary principle should be "cost effective". There is no way of appropriately judging cost effectiveness unless environmental and social costs are included in the cost-benefit analysis.

Principle 16, dealing with internalisation of environmental costs and the polluter pays principle, is also heavily qualified. It says that internalisation of environmental costs should take due regard of the public interest, and should not distort international trade and investment. The qualifiers to the precautionary principle were added by the United States.

Principle 17 urges the use of environmental impact assessment (EIA), which is useful but falls short of best practice. Many observers feel that there is now a need to adapt EIA to include social

Above: One of the hundreds of thousands of personal pledges which adorned the Tree of Life.

and participatory factors – a so-called sustainability analysis.

Principles 20, 21, and 22 address a number of the major groups. Principle 20 is a testament to the impressive power of the women's lobby, as Principle 21 is to youth. Indigenous peoples, like women and youth, are recognised by Principle 22 for their vital role in environmental management and development, and states are called upon to recognise their culture, identity and interests. But referring to indigenous peoples (which recognises the diversity, autonomy, and self-determined nature of different peoples), as "indigenous people and their communities" subtly undermines their socio-political status. Taken together, Principles 20 to 22 and the Major Groups chapter of *Agenda 21*, are seen by some as the acceptance and emergence of international civil society.

Principle 23, which referred to peoples under occupation, is a straight piece of politicking between Israel and the Arab states, and nearly prompted Israel to pull out of the Summit. The United States attempted to remove any references to war. However, Principle 24 contains the principle that warfare is inherently destructive of sustainable development. But far from condemning weapons of mass destruction or discouraging war *per se* (as Stockholm did), the principle only weakly calls for a sticking to the rules of the game in respect to the environment and war. This is small cheer to the hundreds of thousands of people whose development efforts are continually undermined by other peoples' conflicts.

Conversely, the statement in Principle 25 that "Peace, development and environmental protection are interdependent and indivisible", appears stronger than the Stockholm statements.

The overall message is somewhat ambiguous. Is it green war or no war? Principle 26, on environmental disputes, goes no further than existing documents. This is surprising, since in many respects the whole of the Earth Summit is about environmental security.

Principle 27 closes the declaration by stating that "States and people shall cooperate in good faith and in a spirit of partnership in the fulfilment of the principles embodied in this Declaration".

Discussion

Agenda 21's preamble says that the agenda will be carried out in full respect of all the principles in the Rio Declaration. But how seriously will governments and others treat the Rio Declaration? It is certainly not hard law in respect to being in any way binding. Some governments felt that the declaration could push forward the boundaries of what should be law. Some in business treat it very seriously, noting the tendency (for example, in the European Community) for soft law to be used as a lever to develop or promote binding legislation. Indeed, some countries are even talking about a process to translate the Earth Charter, or parts of it, into law.

At an international level, it seems certain that it would be a very tough struggle indeed to make the Rio Declaration any more explicit. For many, the Rio Declaration was a damage limitation exercise; for others, it was an attempt to establish new precedents or springboards for future negotiation. It might be that the Rio Declaration will be applied and interpreted nationally, or in the case of the European Community, regionally. Since the Rio Declaration was the first global statement of certain principles, for example the polluter pays principle, it doubtless will be quoted in many future UN negotiations.

The Rio Declaration is far from inspirational. It is predominantly sociopolitical in content, and not as

ecological as some may have wished. It is a typical piece of UN New York negotiation, which some claim reduces every principle to the lowest common denominator.

NGOs would also have preferred a text which emphasised "thou shalt" rather than "thou shalt not". At a national level, the utility of the Rio Declaration will be strongly country specific. Cynics would say that for progressive nations, it is very weak, and for those who are not progressive, there are sufficient qualifiers to get out of any real commitment. It will take a very committed and persistent civil society to move things forward with the Rio Declaration as a tool. Optimists will point to the spirit of participation and local action. Historians will note the Rio Declaration as a brutish distillation of the conflicts between the priorities of the rich North and the poorer South; the tensions between self-centred nationalism and sovereignty, and the necessity for cooperation and partnership imposed by our sharing one small and threatened Earth.

It is often asked whether the Rio Declaration represents progress from the Stockholm Declaration of Principles. This is not an easy question to answer, and perhaps is inappropriate in itself. The Rio Declaration is different in function and emphasis, and can only be understood in the political context within which it was written. Development is the stronger theme in the Rio Declaration, whereas environment and even wildlife issues dominate in the Stockholm Principles.

The spirit of what might be called "Only One Earth" is stronger in the Stockholm Principles, and sovereignty is not mentioned until Principle 21. The Stockholm Principles have undoubtedly influenced the development of international environmental law. But whereas the emphasis was on stating the problem of environmental decline, and elaborating mechanisms to deal with it, the problems of the Rio Declaration are more to do with implementation, blame, and responsibility.

A detailed comparison would end up with a very complex score card. Neither can be interpreted outside of the then current political context. Although trade issues were major concerns in 1972, the debt crisis did not emerge until ten years later, and although poverty was severe then, the present gap between rich and poor is even greater. Political dividing lines have changed too: whereas Cold War politics set the geopolitical stage in 1972, the politics of rich and poor have replaced them twenty years later.

Maurice Strong expressed a hope that the Rio Declaration could be developed into an Earth Charter for the 50th Anniversary of the UN in 1995. In Chapter 39 of *Agenda 21* it is suggested that states might look at the feasibility of elaborating general rights and obligations in the field of environment and development, and perhaps this is the direction in which the new Earth Charter will move.

7: A Guide to Agenda 21

Agenda 21 was envisaged as the programme for implementing the principles enunciated in the Earth Charter, which later became the Rio Declaration. The agenda was meant to offer clearly articulated objectives, targets, strategies, activities, costings and an allocation of institutional roles. It is based on the potential areas for action identified in the documents on the sectoral and cross-sectoral issues debated in the Prepcoms.

The Secretary-General's report to Prepcom 3 stressed that *Agenda 21* was essentially a modified version of action plans endorsed by past UN conferences. However, there were some significant differences arising out of the complex and comprehensive mandate for the conference in UN General Assembly resolution 44/228, namely that:

■ the environment and development aspects of each issue should be dealt with on an integrated basis,
■ the cross-sectoral aspects of each issue must be examined separately and reflected in an examination of the issues themselves (examples of cross-sectoral aspects include poverty, human resource development, consumption, financial resources) and

■ significant linkages between issues should be identified and their implications made clear.

Even a cursory examination of the vast array of issues covered made it clear early on in the UNCED process that *Agenda 21* would have to be a comprehensive and complex document. But its scope began to become apparent only late in the process, after Prepcom 3. In its final form, it has 40 chapters spread over some 500 pages. It covers virtually every important issue related to environment and development, some less helpful than others. It is a document negotiated by government civil servants, most of whom had little personal expertise in the issues involved. The political controversies were substantial, and final consensus was reached only with considerable difficulty. This is important to emphasise, since it explains many of the strengths as well as the weaknesses of the document.

The chapters are divided into four sections:

1 Social and economic dimensions;
2 Conservation and management of resources for development;
3 Strengthening the role of major groups;
4 Means of implementation.

Section 1 covers major underlying cross-cutting issues (poverty, demography, trade, economics etc) and section 2 the sectoral issues (forestry, agriculture, oceans, atmosphere, wastes etc). The "major groups" in Section 3 include women, youth, farmers, and NGOs. Section 4 deals with issues like financial resources, technology transfer, capacity building and international institutions. A complete list of the chapters in *Agenda 21*, and their main contents, is provided in appendix 2.

Most of the chapters divide into programmes, although some chapters contain only one programme. For each programme there are sections on

■ basis for action
■ objectives
■ activities
■ means of implementation.

The section on means of implementation contains subheadings on finance and costs, scientific and technological means,

Top: Pupils aged four to sixty attend the Chico Mendes school in the Amazon.

human resource development and capacity building, with modifications as appropriate.

Agenda 21 has a preamble that is important in setting its context. What is its status? Is it a mere declaration of good intent? Should it be implemented, or just used as a guideline? And who should do what?

A key clause in the preamble says that Agenda 21 "reflects a global consensus and political commitment at the highest level on development and environment cooperation". In UN terms, short of tough language on real and binding commitment, "political commitment at the highest level" is the best you can get. In practice, national leaders will only be held accountable through peer and public pressure.

As a secretariat paper for Prepcom 3 put it, "although not legally binding in nature, approval of Agenda 21 by UNCED would represent a high degree of political commitment which would provide the basis for the necessary complementary and supportive action...". As with other UN consensus resolutions, Agenda 21 is only worth what national governments are prepared to make it worth.

The principal concepts of Agenda 21

Maurice Strong remarked on several occasions that the fundamental issues for UNCED were the inequities between rich and poor, wasteful consumption patterns, the population explosion, and the need to integrate environmental concerns into mainstream economic decision-making. This line of thought is clearly reflected in Section 1, the seven chapters on social and economic dimensions that provide the conceptual core of Agenda 21. This is arguably the most important part of the document.

The first chapter deals with international economic issues with the rationale that sustainable development will be difficult to pursue unless the international economic climate is supportive. The chapter therefore deals with trade, debt, financial flows and the macroeconomic policy framework. The main purpose here is to highlight the linkage between these issues and sustainable development.

The three following chapters dealing with poverty, consumption patterns and population provide the analytical centrepiece. Nitin Desai, the Deputy Secretary-General of UNCED, has suggested that "the objectives included in these programme areas represent the hard core of the transition to sustainability". He points out that, with

regard to poverty, Agenda 21 seeks to combine two strands of development action, one which focuses attention on improving the access of the poor to the resources that they need for survival and development, and one which concentrates on management of these resources. These two strands need to be woven together to ensure that anti-poverty programmes have in them an element of natural resource management, and that resource management programmes include in them an element of improved access to these resources by the poor.

References to poverty and to the need to empower the poor to participate more actively in programmes to protect the environment recur throughout Agenda 21 and are one of its principal themes. The document therefore calls for a fresh look at approaches to deal with poverty and environment. There are in various chapters several references to "primary environmental care", a methodology to meet basic needs through empowerment of communities to protect their own environment.

The chapter on consumption patterns essentially recognises that this area presents problems for the global environment and that "all countries should strive to promote sustainable consumption patterns". Some first steps towards the assessment and tackling of this intractable problem are presented, but the text is weak. The United States, often supported by Japan, consistently tried to water it down even further to reduce the responsibility attributed to rich nations for unsustainable consumption patterns.

A key chapter on demographic factors follows. It emphasises that the growth of world population in combination with unsustainable consumption patterns places increasingly severe stress on the global environment, affecting the use of land, water, air, energy and other resources. This chapter contains concrete recommendations for integrated action programmes at the local level that are consistent with the approaches advocated to tackle poverty. Desai stresses that these three programme areas – poverty, consumption patterns, and demographic pressures – provide the organising principles for the sectoral chapters of Agenda 21, and are much reflected in them.

An assessment of Agenda 21

It is a pity that this grand design underlying Agenda 21 is not highlighted more clearly in the preamble, because it will be lost on many readers. The document certainly represents a very brave attempt to draw up a master plan for environment and development well into the next century. However, since it sets out to be all-encompassing, it inevitably becomes complex; and since it is a negotiated UN text, it makes for difficult and tedious reading.

The main achievement of Agenda 21 is that it provides a comprehensive inventory of the issues pertinent to sustainable development, highlights linkages between them, and suggests principal action programmes. As such, it provides an important framework and point of reference for future work. No doubt there will be attempts to refine its analytical approach in coming years and improvements on parts or all of it. Nevertheless, it constitutes a significant point of departure for intensified efforts to put the world on a more sustainable path of development. This is an important outcome, given the difficulties of steering this text through the negotiating process. Much credit goes to the conference organisers, primarily the conference chairman, Tommy Koh from Singapore.

It would be fatuous to try to list what Agenda 21 leaves out. Even if most major issues are covered, one can always claim that some aspect has been left out. One can argue endlessly about the coverage of individual chapters and about the perspectives adopted. Clearly, some chapters are better and less ambiguous than others, depending on the issues involved and on the controversies they caused during negotiations. For example, chapter 8 on the linkage between environment and economics was never controversial and is clear and succinct, while chapter 4 on consumption was much debated and is vague and unspecific. But some overriding points may be made.

First, from the point of view of the developing countries, Agenda 21 represents a climb-down and a disappointment in terms of the original conference objectives stated in UN General Assembly resolution 44/228. As Adil Najam has pointed out, "Agenda 21 is weakest on the very things that 44/228 stressed the most: financial arrangements, institutional arrangements, and technology transfer". He suggests that Rio did not take these issues any further than the UN environment conference in Stockholm 20 years earlier.

Second, the principal shortcoming of Agenda 21 is that it is not funded. Prepcom 3 requested the conference secretariat to provide full cost estimates, but it is doubtful whether this could ever have been done in a meaningful way. The cost estimated by the secretariat, in total some US$600 billion annually of which US$125 billion was to be covered by foreign aid, was a totally unrealistic figure in terms of the actual money which would materialise. Since all were aware of the wide error margins in these estimates, it was not a good basis for serious debate. The current political climate in the donor countries is not conducive to increased aid flows, let alone huge increases based on uncertain estimates. In that it is unfinanced, Agenda 21 can always be dismissed by critics as a meaningless pile of paper.

Third, there is no attempt to set priorities; everything seems equally important (a chronic shortcoming of UN documents). It is possible to surmise the priorities from the first chapters; certainly poverty eradication is obviously and very rightly held out as a priority. But these unstated priorities should have been stated and stated clearly. There is no attempt to define the relative scale of the issues involved nor of the action programmes proposed. This tends to reinforce the impression that it is a paper exercise, a plan in need of much more refinement before it can be called operationally useful.

Fourth, the emphasis on poverty leading to environmental problems obscures the fact that it is in many cases inequity and pursuit of wealth, often by the richer countries and societal groups, which cause more serious problems – including poverty itself. In the references to poverty-related programmes there is much use of the word "community" but little recognition of the conflict and the lack of homogeneity found within many communities.

Fifth, many of the statements concerning the need for redistribution of land to the poor and empowerment of communities are poorly grounded in practical experience and in the *realpolitik* of many countries. More equitable ownership of land would certainly be conducive to sustainable development but remains a pipedream in many countries. Further, many of the recommendations – for example on "accelerated afforestation and reforestation programmes" in arid lands – fly in the face of a largely negative practical experience. In the absence of any explicit recognition of implementation difficulties, the document at times gives an impression of naïvety.

Sixth, there is great emphasis throughout *Agenda 21*, in chapter 38 and elsewhere, on the "unique position" of the UN system in implementing the agenda. It is useful to remember that bilateral disbursements of aid over the last several years have been 3-4 times higher than multilateral disbursement. As underlined by recent studies, the UN system is often inefficient, disorganised, and in dire need of improvement. Perhaps it is inevitable that *Agenda 21* has a strong UN focus, but some recognition of the role and abilities of the UN system relative to other international and national actors would not have been out of place.

A concluding assessment of *Agenda 21* would be that it should be seen as a valuable first step in a process to gradually refine international cooperation towards a more sustainable world. It may even provide an important framework for such work.

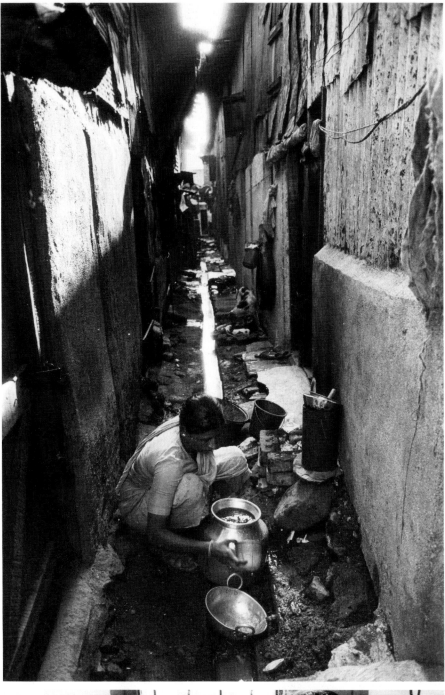

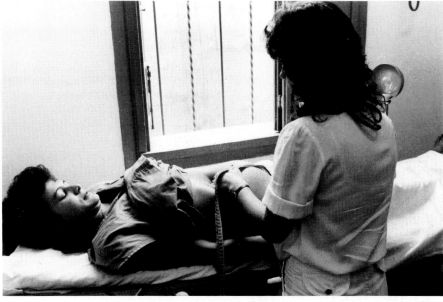

Right: Tackling population problems through better maternity and child care in Rio.
Top: Health challenges for *Agenda 21*: washing dishes in open drains in Bombay.

8: UN Institutions: New Partnerships for Sustainable Development?

UNCED's most visible new institutional product is the UN Commission on Sustainable Development. But associated with the Rio Conference are several less tangible institutional developments that could accelerate the integration of environmental protection with economic development, and enhance quality of life.

First, *Agenda 21's* conceptual framework recognises the many ways in which economic, social, and environmental forces interact. It promotes national strategies to give concrete meaning to sustainable development, and it offers a structure for organising international policies and programmes when the issues involved have regional or global consequences. The old sector-by-sector, project-by-project approach of international institutions must yield to new organising principles.

Second, UNCED acknowledged, in spirit and in practice, that the UN family of organisations is today supplemented by many regional and treaty organisations, and that "major groups" such as women and youth will more and more complement and extend the activities sponsored by inter-governmental organisations. This should result in increasingly varied and flexible alliances that make the most of the skills and resources of each participating organisation or group, internationally as well as nationally. At the same time, scarce financing for international assistance and the interactive nature of the problems require better planning from the outset, so that multilateral and bilateral donors do not work at cross purposes. *Agenda 21* provides a tool for mobilising and coordinating the efforts of the international system as a whole, and establishes a framework for other actors to collectively reinforce.

Third, the Rio Conference has finally reinstated the environment/development agenda as an essential element in creating "conditions of stability and well-being which are necessary for peaceful and friendly relations among nations". As reiterated by UN Secretary-General Boutros-Ghali in his speech before the UN Economic and Social Council in July 1992:

"it is futile, if not counterproductive, to separate out the political and the economic and social missions of the [UN] Organisation.... An integrated approach to cooperation in these areas... needs, however, to be pondered and emphasised anew, after decades of increasing fragmentation of structures and mandates. The concepts of peace-building and preventive diplomacy must be viewed in that light."

The 47th session of the UN General Assembly (GA) took up the results of UNCED when it convened in September 1992. It faced several specific tasks in following up the international institutional arrangements agreed in chapter 38 of *Agenda 21* and related sections. But the agenda of reform inspired in part by UNCED will continue well beyond that gathering.

The Commission on Sustainable Development: The Commission is to begin meeting in 1993, with a mandate to review progress in the implementation of *Agenda 21* at national, regional, and global levels, and to rationalise inter-governmental decision-making on environment and development issues. The GA will work out the organisational details of the Commission, including its membership, its relationship to other UN bodies – such as UNEP and UNDP – its staffing and finances, and the frequency, duration and location of its meetings.

The GA's challenge will be to produce a mandate for the Commission that grants it the leeway to evolve and adapt to the changing needs of sustainable development. The Commission should update *Agenda 21* and set new goals when these are required. At the same time, it is up to each government to strive for greater consistency in the positions it espouses in different international organisations. The Commission cannot succeed in bringing order out of this chaos unless governments take the initiative. That will require continuity and expertise on the part of those who represent their governments in the Commission, as well as credibility at home. The Commission, in its review of the implementation of *Agenda 21*, presents a useful vehicle for achieving that consistency, and NGOs should insist on it.

The Commission's role as a watchdog should be channelled in constructive directions. It should help pinpoint the reasons why governments neglect their commitments, such as insufficient financial resources, inappropriate technologies, or difficulties in determining appropriate regulatory policies. By drawing attention to these deficiencies, it can help mobilise constructive responses.

Only when these failures represent a consistent pattern or constitute a serious violation should the Commission consider more intrusive investigatory action. Otherwise, leave it to authoritative, independent assessments and to NGOs to bring pressure to bear. And if the documentation prepared for the Commission clearly juxtaposes objectives and accomplishments, it may shame the reluctant into action.

When it comes to international institutions, the Commission should seriously consider how to establish a process for periodic, independent review of their policies and programmes to make sure that they reinforce sustainable development. It is unrealistic to assume that reports prepared by these agencies will illustrate their own shortcomings. The reports should be used to identify new issues and problems and to concert programme efforts.

The Commission's Secretariat: It is up to Boutros-Ghali to determine the secretariat staffing arrangements for the new Commission and the reinvigorated inter-agency coordination process. He will have to keep two essential requirements in mind: the secretariat must be independent enough to muster and channel the energy demonstrated by Maurice Strong's UNCED secretariat, and it must be installed at the centre of the UN power structure for economic, social/environment, and development affairs. These requirements might argue the case for a senior staff director with an overview of related UN programmes such as UNEP and UNDP, reporting directly to the Secretary-General. Otherwise, the Commission will become yet another UN appendage, and its inter-agency coordination efforts will carry little weight with relevant UN agencies and programmes. Boutros-Ghali has indicated that these staffing issues will be dealt with in his next stage of measures to enhance the effectiveness and coherence of the UN's economic and social structure.

The UN General Assembly: The General Assembly may convene, no later than 1997, a special session to review and appraise *Agenda 21*. During the 1992 GA session, governments were called upon to report their plans and commitments for making available financial resources to support the decisions taken at Rio. Similar sessions could be used regularly to promote more secure and predictable investments in "preventive diplomacy".

In his July presentation to the UN Economic and Social Council (ECOSOC), Maurice Strong suggested that a high-level consultative panel be associated with the Commission to facilitate the review and monitoring of financial resources for implementing *Agenda 21*. Such a panel would be particularly useful were it to associate all major bilateral and multilateral donors, together with large private foundations and private corporations. Its preparatory work with the Commission could be followed up by regular pledging sessions in the GA.

The international inter-agency structure: Secretary-General Boutros-Ghali is not taking lightly his statement that fragmented mandates need "pondering anew". Following the conclusion of UNCED, he established a task force, chaired by FAO Director General Saouma, to examine the UN system-wide implications arising from UNCED, and asked for a review of how to improve the structure and functioning of inter-agency coordination.

He also established a panel of high-level, independent experts to advise him on the future course of UN development activities, including follow-up to UNCED. The panel is co-chaired by Jan Pronk, Minister of Development Cooperation of the Netherlands, and Enrique Iglesias of Uruguay, President of the Inter-American Development Bank. Their advice will be considered this autumn.

If the UN inter-agency process can be reconstructed to foster mutually-reinforcing activities among different UN and non-UN agencies, this will be a major step in improving the inter-governmental system's response to the needs of sustainable development. Equally critical is the order of activities. The agencies must report to the Commission and ECOSOC in sufficient time for these two bodies to integrate planning and coordination. The individual sectoral agencies must act and report; then the Commission must review the adequacy of these activities; then ECOSOC plans the integration and coordination of these activities, taking account of the Commission's assessment; then ECOSOC and the General Assembly give the agencies additional direction. If this sequence cannot be followed efficiently, the system will have little value.

UN Development Programme and UN Environment Programme: UNCED has recommended that UNDP take the lead in concentrating the efforts of the UN system for capacity-building. In doing so, UNDP will have to foster new alliances with multilateral and bilateral donors that pay close attention to education and training, infrastructure, data collection, research, and policy analysis capabilities. These issues will be considered by the Secretary-General's new expert panel. UNEP has in principle been strengthened by UNCED, but in reality no new resources are pledged for its environmental assessment and environmental policy-making. Its technical cooperation role will have to be worked out in the larger context addressed by the expert panel.

The Global Environment Facility (GEF) is likely to play a key role in future funding for global environmental problems, including the environmental monitoring and assessment necessary to underpin viable solutions. It represents a major new partnership between the World Bank, two UN agencies (UNDP and UNEP), and the signatories to international agreements on ozone, climate, and biodiversity. It may in future help spawn similar partnerships with other UN agencies, international treaties, and regional and bilateral donors. In December 1992, the countries participating in the GEF were to make another attempt at revising its governance, so as to meet the conditions prescribed in the treaties and *Agenda 21*: universal participation, balanced and equitable representation of developing a nation's interests, and due weight to the funding efforts of donor countries.

The information base and expert advice: *Agenda 21* emphasises the need for more sophisticated early warning systems and more extensive scientific and technical assessments. Without these analytical foundations, policy-makers will be unable to anticipate and respond to emerging problems, and it will be difficult to build international consensus around viable solutions. *Agenda 21* would strengthen Earthwatch, the UN inter-agency environmental monitoring program coordinated by UNEP, and establish a new Development Watch to coordinate economic and social statistics and assessments. These two would be linked through an appropriate, and yet to be identified, UN office.

Secretary-General Boutros-Ghali was called upon to make recommendations to the 47th GA on the appointment of a high-level board of eminent persons, who would advise him on environment and development issues. *Agenda 21* also suggests the need for different inter-governmental panels comprised of multi-disciplinary experts, along the lines of the Inter-governmental Panel on Climate Change (IPCC).

The needs of the UN system and other inter-governmental institutions for expert advice and analysis must be carefully thought through, and priorities established. Perhaps that should be the first task of the "eminent persons" group. In doing so, the group must seek out the most effective means by which inter-governmental expert panels, international organisation staff, and non-governmental bodies can meet these needs. This exercise must acknowledge that authoritative, impartial views can only be obtained if both governmental and non-governmental experts are subject to independent peer review.

Regional concentration: The fabric of international cooperation would be greatly enhanced if better use were made of the UN system's regional and national offices, and if they would sort out their comparative advantages with regard to autonomous regional organisations. *Agenda 21* emphasises the regional roles of UNDP, UNEP, the UN regional economic commissions, and the regional development banks. It also holds out the prospect of regional consultative mechanisms that would include NGOs and all relevant donors. These would exchange development experiences, review implementation of *Agenda 21*, and harmonise donor programmes.

As a first step, the UN Secretary-General is to survey UNCED's many recommendations for regional information networks and other capacity-building programmes, and for regional policies and programmes to deal with transboundary resources and ecosystems. His new panel of development experts will contribute to this effort.

The Commission on Sustainable Development will then consider this survey and its implications for improved regional cooperation. Regional focal points will most likely represent the wave of the future in international institution-building for several reasons: in keeping with the principle of subsidiarity, as more and more issues of sustainable development transgress national boundaries, and as comprehensive global frameworks require building blocks adapted to specific economic, social, and environmental attributes.

Non-governmental actors: *Agenda 21* calls for all inter-governmental organisations (which were called non-governmental actors at Rio), including the international finance and development agencies, to reconsider their procedures so that NGOs can better contribute to policy design, decision-making, implementation, and evaluation. It says that accreditation procedures should be based on those used in UNCED, and it provides specifically for the Commission to receive and analyse relevant input from competent NGOs.

The establishment of the Sustainable Development Commission should provide the first opportunity to give effect to these decisions. The possibility of full partnership or "associated" membership status for the different major groups should be given serious consideration. Equally important, new procedures will have to be worked out to make available relevant information and documentation from UN bodies to these constituencies in a timely manner. Otherwise, they will be unable to participate effectively.

9: Success at Rio? A Dialogue

Optimist: It was a real achievement that governments got together to discuss environment and development at such a high level. Surely now there can be no world leader who can claim ignorance or lack of awareness of the issues.

Pessimist: But governments have been talking for 20 years about problems of environment and development. The point now is to turn words into action.

Optimist: It is a major achievement that governments realise the inter-connectedness between environment and development. Now they cannot speak of one without having to speak of the other.

Pessimist: I thought that governments signed on to this idea in 1987 with the report of the World Commission on Environment and Development – the so-called Brundtland Commission – and again later in 1989 in the enabling resolution 44/228. Strong said that the Earth Summit would turn the WCED Report into committed action.

Optimist: It must be an achievement that we got agreements at all. Just before Rio, things looked very bad indeed – in terms of getting any agreements.

Pessimist: Getting agreement is the diplomat's measure of success, irrespective – it seems – of content. The UN negotiation process, bound by the need for consensus, has delivered the lowest common denominator of agreement. Besides, you must know that government representatives came to Rio with very restrictive briefs, with orders to concede very little, and where possible agree process rather than action. The progressives have been dragged down and their words watered down. The Earth Summit agreements reflect present disagreements rather than future solutions. Norwegian Prime Minister Gro Harlem Brundtland said that the Earth Summit achieved little progress in some areas, some progress in other areas, and no progress in others. She implied that this was not good enough, and we will have to investigate new ways to make decisions on the international stage.

Optimist: We have achieved a real commitment towards an evolutionary process of change. We are taking first steps.

Pessimist: We are always taking the first step. When are we going to take the next step? Didn't we take the first step in Stockholm in 1972, and then again in 1987, and again in 1989? Are we

seeing a calculated diplomatic alchemy which is turning pure action into base process?

Optimist: As a result of the Earth Summit we are moving into a new era of North-South partnership, one based upon mutual goals and cooperation.

Pessimist: The Earth Summit was characterised by North-South conflict, which now that the East-West conflict has dimmed will dominate world politics for years to come. There was little indication that the rich countries wished to help the poorer countries to accelerate their development, or to make concessions on debt, trade and financial flows. We are a million miles away from a mature and equitable North-South partnership.

Optimist: But at least we have realised the seriousness of the problem.

Pessimist: The fact that patterns of consumption and development must change so that human and economic activity stays within ecological constraints was hardly discussed. It was hardly acknowledged that there were constraints, certainly not ones within the foreseeable future.

Optimist: I concede some of your points, but it serves no purpose, save a self-serving one, to write the Earth Summit off. It is simply too early to judge progress. We must look to the UN General Assembly meeting in late 1992 and the development of the Sustainable Development Commission, the

replenishment of World Bank funds, and the outcome of national processes in one or two years' time to make judgements. Nations have committed themselves to participatory national sustainable development plans and strategies, which can only be good. The principle of subsidiarity is firmly established, as is the whole concept of participatory development, and issues of "governance for sustainable development" are firmly on the agenda. NGOs now have opportunities to influence events in an unprecedented way. Women's organisations have achieved nearly all their objectives in relation to *Agenda 21*, and major parts of *Agenda 21* were written by NGOs. Much of the Earth Summit's success will come about because institutions and organisations will commit themselves to follow-up and implementation, making full use of the many levers and opportunities in *Agenda 21*. In terms of *realpolitik*, in a time of recession, the competition for resources in Eastern Europe and the former Soviet Union, and more conservative, inward-looking governments, what more could you expect? Get real!

Pessimist: Get real? You judge progress by what governments can be expected to do. I judge progress by planetary needs. What could be more real than that?

However you judge the Earth Summit, the work starts now to put some reality behind its words.

Above: Homeless in Lagos, Nigeria.

Appendix 1
Targets and Timetables: What Rio agreed to do

Action plans are not new to the United Nations system. Maurice Strong in conceiving *Agenda 21* was well aware of the UN's past record with action plans; they line the shelves or fill bins. His solution was to back each objective in *Agenda 21* with clear targets, schedules for achieving them, and money to make it happen. This "green strait jacket" would bind governments to their commitments. But the diplomats at the Prepcoms and at Rio saw to it that things did not work out quite so neatly.

Many critics of *Agenda 21* claim that it contains no targets. This is not true. Although the language of commitment is often highly qualified, there are many real targets for the next 10 years and more.

This appendix describes those targets. Not every chapter of *Agenda 21* contains targets. But the targets within *Agenda 21* are just a few of the hundreds of commitments made. If a chapter contains many targets, this does not necessarily imply that the subject will be given a higher priority. Indeed, some highly generalised objectives are already being pursued by governments and the UN.

For those whose business it is to pressure governments to stick by their promises, this list should prove a valuable tool. It may also prove useful to those inside government who would like to honour their own and their colleagues' promises.

The most serious obstacle to meeting any of the targets is the lack of money to fund *Agenda 21*. It is commonly understood, and explicitly stated in *Agenda 21*, that fulfilment of targets will depend upon new and additional financial resources. They do not appear to be on the horizon.

Targets

The 1990s were designated The International Decade for Natural Disaster Reduction. Goals include the following:

1992 to 1995
■ 1992: the 47th Session of the UN General Assembly. Negotiations will include decisions on institutional follow-up within the UN generally and the establishment of the Sustainable Development Commission; donor reports on finance; and setting-up of the Intergovernmental Negotiating Committee for a Desertification Convention.
■ a "Like-minded" Fisheries Conference in Newfoundland, to include discussion of controversial "straddling stocks".
■ Climate Convention Meeting, USA (by 1 Jan 1993).
■ negotiation of a new International Tropical Timber Agreement.

■ in the realm of education "Governments should strive to update or prepare strategies aimed at integrating environment and development as a cross-cutting issue into education at all levels within the next three years (1992-5)". (36.5.a)
■ a Global conference on the Sustainable Development of Small Island Developing States in 1993. (17.131)
■ adoption of the International Labour Organisation Instrument on the Prevention of Industrial Disasters. (19.47)
■ International Year for the World's Indigenous People. (26.2)
■ Technology Partnership Conference, UK.
■ NGO Conference on implementation of *Agenda 21*, UK.
■ Coastal Zone Management Conference, Netherlands.
■ Wetlands Conference, Turkey.
■ First Conference of the Parties to the Climate Convention, Germany (late 1993/early 1994).
■ Convening of the Sustainable Development Commission.
■ by 1993, "Establish procedures allowing for consultation and possible participation of youth of both genders . . . in decision-making processes with regard to the environment, involving youth at the local, national and regional levels". (25.9.a)
■ by the same year, "The international community should have initiated a consultative process aimed at increasing cooperation between local authorities". (28.2.b)
■ desertification negotiations should be completed by June 1994.
■ International Conference on Population and Development (1994) "Governments could share their experience in the implementation of *Agenda 21*".
■ in 1994 there should be a fourth International Technical Conference on the Conservation and Sustainable Use of Plant Genetic Resources for Agriculture. (14.60.e)
■ by 1994 "Representatives of associations of cities and other local authorities should have increased levels of cooperation and coordination with the goal of enhancing the exchange of information and experience among local authorities". (28.2.c)
■ by the same year "The UN system should undertake a comprehensive review of its educational priorities..." (36.5.g), and
■ carry out a "Review of capacity – and capability requirements for devising national sustainable development strategies". (37.4.a)
■ 1995 will be the 50th Anniversary of UN System. To mark the occasion, there should be development of the Earth Charter, and a World Conference on Women. (24.3)

There are additional targets in the following areas:

Agriculture:
"By 1995, to review and where appropriate establish a programme to integrate environmental and sustainable development with policy analysis for the food and agricultural sector and relevant macroeconomic policy analysis, formulation and implementation." (14.8.a)
Solid Wastes and Sewage:
"In industrialised countries, and by the year 2005 in developing countries, ensure that at least 50 per cent of all sewage, waste waters and solid wastes are treated or disposed of in conformity with national or international environmental and health guidelines." (21.29.c)
Women:
"To establish mechanisms at the national, regional and international levels to assess the implementation and impact of development and environment policies and programmes on women and to ensure their contributions and benefits." (24.2.c)
NGOs:
"A mutually productive dialogue should be established at the national level between all Governments and NGOs and their self-organised networks to recognise and strengthen their respective roles in implementing environmentally sound and sustainable development." (27.7)
Education/Training:
"A review of progress in (identifying workforce training needs and measures to be taken to meet those needs) could be undertaken by the UN system." (36.14)
Health:
"By 1995 (...) reduce measles deaths by 95 per cent and reduce measles cases by 90 per cent compared with pre-immunisation levels."

1995 to 2000
Land Resources:
"Review and develop policies to support the best possible use of land and sustainable management of land resources, by not later than 1996." (10.5.a)
"Create mechanisms to facilitate the active involvement and participation of all concerned, particularly communities and local people at the local level, in decision-making on land use and management, by not later than 1996." (10.5.d)
Local Authorities:
"Most local authorities in each country (by 1996) should have undertaken a consultative process with their

populations and achieved a consensus on a "local *Agenda 21*" for their community." (28.2.a)

Education:
"To strengthen information exchange... to promote environment and development education and public awareness (by 1996)." (36.5.a)

Capacity Building:
"The Secretary General of the UN should submit to the General Assembly (by 1997) a report on the achievement of improved policies, coordinate systems and procedures for strengthening the implementation of technical cooperation programmes for sustainable development, as well as additional measures required to strengthen such cooperation." (37.4.b)

Institutions:
"The General Assembly should consider holding a special session no later than 1997 for the purpose of overall review and appraisal of *Agenda 21*." (38.9)

Land Resources:
"Strengthen institutions and coordinating mechanisms for land and land resources, by not later than 1998." (10.5.c)

Agriculture:
"Maintain and develop as appropriate, operational multisectoral plans, programmes and policy measures to enhance sustainable food production and food security, within the framework of sustainable development, not later than 1998." (14.8.b)
"Not later than 1998, (...) establish operational and interactive networks among farmers, researchers and extension services to promote and develop integrated pest management." (14.75.c)
Other targets were set for the end of the millenia, and are divided by subject area below.

Human Settlements targets urge that:
"During the period 1993-2000, all countries should undertake, with the active participation of the business sector as appropriate, pilot projects in selected cities for the collection, analysis and subsequent dissemination of urban data, including environmental impact analysis at the local, state/provincial, national and international levels..." (7.17)
"...all developing countries incorporate in their national strategies programmes to build the necessary technical, financial and human resource capacity aimed at ensuring better integration of infrastructure and environmental planning by the year 2000." (7.38)
"Strengthening the development of human resources and of capacities of public sector institutions through technical assistance and international cooperation so as to achieve by the year 2000 substantial improvement in the efficiency of governmental activities." (7.77.a)

Health: the overall strategy is "to achieve health for all by the year 2000." (6.4)
Within that strategy, there are targets to:
■ eliminate Guinea Worm disease.
■ eradicate polio.
■ effectively control river blindness and leprosy.
and reduce:
■ the number of deaths from childhood diarrhoea in developing countries by at least 50-70 per cent.
■ the incidence of childhood diarrhoea in developing countries by at least 25-50 per cent.

Agenda 21 also urges participants to:
■ initiate comprehensive programmes to reduce mortality from acute respiratory infections in children under five years by at least one third.
■ provide 95 per cent of the world's child population with access to appropriate care for acute respiratory infections within the community and at first referral level.
■ institute anti-malaria programmes in all countries where malaria presents a significant health problem.
■ implement control programmes in countries where major human parasitic infections are endemic and achieve an overall reduction in the prevalence of schistosomiasis and of other trematode infections by 40 per cent and 25 per cent respectively, from a 1984 baseline, as well as a marked reduction in incidence, prevalence and intensity of filarial infections. (6.12.a-i)
■ mobilise and unify national and international efforts against AIDS to prevent infection and to reduce the personal and social impact of HIV infection.
■ contain the resurgence of tuberculosis.
■ accelerate research on improved vaccines.
Overall "The global objective is to achieve a 10-40 per cent improvement in health indicators by the year 2000." (6.34)

Health risks from environmental pollution and hazards: by the year 2000, measures should have been taken to:
"incorporate appropriate environmental health safeguards as part of national development programmes in all countries",
"establish, as appropriate, adequate national infrastructure programmes for providing environmental injury, hazard surveillance and the basis for abatement in all countries",
"establish, as appropriate, integrated programmes for tackling pollution at the source and at the disposal site, with a focus on abatement actions in all countries",
"identify and compile as appropriate, the necessary statistical information on health effects to support cost/benefit analysis."

Land Resources targets are to:
"Improve and strengthen planning, management and evaluation systems for land and land resources." (10.5.b)

Agriculture objectives are, not later than the year 2000:
"to review and initiate, as appropriate, national land-resource surveys, detailing the location, extent and severity of land degradation", (14.45.a)
"to adopt policies and strengthen or establish programmes for *in-situ* on-farm and *ex-situ* conservation and sustainable use of plant genetic resources for food and agriculture, integrated into programmes for sustainable agriculture", (14.57.c)
"to improve and implement plant protection and animal health services, including mechanisms to control the distribution and use of pesticides, and to implement the International Code of Conduct on the Distribution and Use of Pesticides", (14.75.a)
"to develop and maintain in all countries the integrated plant nutrition approach, and to optimise availability of fertiliser and other plant nutrients", (14.85.a)
"to establish and maintain institutional and human infrastructure to enhance effective decision-making on soil productivity", (14.85.b)
"to initiate and encourage a process of environmentally sound energy transition in rural communities, from unsustainable energy sources, to structured and diversified energy sources by making available new and renewable sources of energy." (14.94.a)

Deforestation targets are:
"By the year 2000, to strengthen the capacities and capabilities of national institutions to enable them to acquire the necessary knowledge for the protection and conservation of forests (...) and enhance the effectiveness of programmes and activities related to the management and development of forests." (11.3.a)

Mountains objectives are:
"By the year 2000, to develop appropriate land-use planning and management for both arable and non-arable land in mountain-fed watershed areas to prevent soil erosion, increase biomass production and maintain ecological balance." (13.15.a)

Freshwater targets are, by the year 2000 to have:
"designed and initiated, costed and targeted, national (freshwater) action

programmes, and have put in place appropriate institutional structures and legal instruments." (18.11.a.i)

"established efficient water-use programmes to attain sustainable resource utilisation patterns." (18.11.a.11)

"studied in detail the feasibility of installing water resources assessment services." (18.26.a)

"ensured that all urban residents have access to at least 40 litres per capita per day of safe water and that 75 per cent of the urban population are provided with on-site or community facilities for sanitation." (18.58.a)

"established and applied quantitative and qualitative discharge standards for municipal and industrial effluents." (18.58.b)

"ensured that 75 per cent of solid waste generated in urban areas is collected and recycled or disposed of in an environmentally safe way." (18.58.c)

Toxic chemicals objectives are:

"To strengthen international risk assessment. Several hundred priority chemicals or groups of chemicals, including major pollutants and contaminants of global significance, should be assessed by the year 2000, using current selection and assessment criteria." (19.13.a)

"A globally harmonised hazard classification and compatible labelling system, including material safety data sheets and easily understandable symbols, should be available if feasible by the year 2000." (19.27)

"To achieve by the year 2000, as feasible, full participation in and implementation of the PIC procedure, including possible mandatory applications through legally binding instruments contained in the Amended London Guidelines and in the FAO International Code of Conduct." (19.38.b)

"By the year 2000, national systems for environmentally sound management of chemicals, including legislation and provisions for implementation and enforcement should be in place in all countries to the extent possible." (19.58)

Solid wastes and sewage objectives in this area are, by the year 2000, to:

"Ensure sufficient national, regional and international capacity to access, process and monitor waste trend information and implement waste minimisation programmes." (21.9.a)

"Have in place in all industrialised countries programmes to stabilise or reduce, if practicable, production of wastes destined for final disposal, including per capita wastes (where this

concept applies), at the level prevailing at that date; developing countries as well should work towards that goal without jeopardising their development prospects." (21.9.b)

"Apply by the year 2000, in all countries, in particular in industrialised countries, programmes to reduce the production of agrochemical wastes, containers and packaging materials, which do not meet hazardous characteristics." (21.9.c)

"Promote sufficient financial and technological capacities at the regional, national and local levels as appropriate, to implement waste reuse and recycling policies and actions." (21.18.a)

"In all industrialised countries, and by the year 2010, in all developing countries, have a national programme, including to the extent possible, targets for efficient waste reuse and recycling." (21.18.b)

"Establish waste treatment and disposal quality criteria, objectives and standards based on the nature and assimilative capacity of the receiving environment." (21.29.a)

"Establish sufficient capacity to undertake waste-related pollution impact monitoring and conduct regular surveillance, including epidemiological surveillance where appropriate." (21.29.b)

"Have the necessary technical, financial and human resource capacity to provide waste collection services..." (21.41.a)

"Have the necessary technical, financial and human resource capacity to provide waste collection services commensurate with needs." (21.39.a)

Women objectives are:

"To consider developing and issuing a strategy of changes necessary to eliminate constitutional, legal and administrative, cultural, behavioural, social and economic obstacles to women's full participation in sustainable development and public life." (24.2.c)

"States party to the Convention on the Elimination of all Forms of Discrimination against Women should review and suggest amendments to it by the year 2000, with a view to strengthening those elements of the Convention related to environment and development..." (24.5)

Youth:

"Each country, by the year 2000, should ensure that more than 50 per cent of its youth, gender balanced, are enrolled in or have access to appropriate secondary education or equivalent educational or vocational training programmes, by increasing participation and access rates on an

annual basis." (25.5)

Workers there should be measures by the year 2000, to:

"promote ratification of relevant conventions of (the) ILO and the enactment of legislation in support of those conventions",

"establish bipartite and tripartite mechanisms on safety, health and sustainable development",

"increase the number of environmental collective agreements aimed at achieving sustainable development",

"reduce occupational accidents, injuries and diseases",

"increase the provision of workers' education, training and retraining, particularly in the area of occupational health and safety and environment". (29.3.a-e)

Science achievements should include:

"A substantial increase in the number of scientists, particularly women scientists, in those developing countries where their number is at present insufficient." (35.21.b)

2000 to 2025

The final group of objectives have more distant target dates. Supporters of Agenda 21 should, by 2005:

"maintain and enhance the ability of developing countries, particularly the least developed ones, to themselves manage (sustainable agricultural) policy, programming and planning activities." (14.8.c)

and

"in developing countries, ensure that at least 50 per cent of all sewage, waste waters and solid wastes are treated or disposed of in conformity with national or international guidelines." (21.30.c)

Solid wastes by 2010 there should be:

"in all developing countries a national programme including targets for efficient waste reuse and recycling." (21.18.b)

Human Settlements by 2025 there should be:

"Provision of adequate environmental infrastructure facilities in all settlements." (7.39)

Freshwater objectives are, by the year 2025:

"To have achieved subsectoral targets of all freshwater programme areas." (18.21.b)

Solid Wastes targets are to:

"Dispose of all sewage, waste water and solid wastes in conformity with national or international environmental quality guidelines", (21.29.d)

"Provide all urban populations with adequate waste services", (21.39.b)

"Ensure that full urban waste service coverage is maintained and sanitation

coverage achieved in rural areas."
(21.39.c)
The following areas have undefined target dates, but clear objectives.

Combating Poverty:
"the long-term objective of enabling all people to achieve sustainable livelihoods...to provide all persons urgently with the opportunity to earn a sustainable livelihood." (3.4.a)

Demographic Dynamics and Sustainability:
"The following objectives should be achieved as soon as practicable:
■ To incorporate demographic trends and factors in the global analysis of environment and development issues;
■ To develop a better understanding of the relationships among demographic dynamics, technology, cultural behaviour, natural resources and life support systems;
■ To assess human vulnerability in ecologically sensitive areas and centres of population to determine the priorities for action at all levels, taking full account of community defined needs."

Sustainable Agriculture:
"Complete the first regeneration and safe duplication of existing *ex situ* collections as soon as possible", (14.57.a) and "Begin a 10-year programme of action." (14.66.a)

Oceans/Marine Resources:
"States should convene, as soon as possible, an intergovernmental conference under UN auspices with a view to promoting effective implementation of the provisions of the UNCLOS on straddling fish stocks and highly migratory fish stocks." (17.52.e)

The following chapters contained no target dates:

1 Preamble
2 International Cooperation
3 Combating Poverty
4 Consumption
8 Decision Making
9 Atmosphere
15 Biodiversity
16 Biotechnology
17 Oceans
20 Hazardous Wastes
22 Radioactive Wastes
30 Business
31 Science Community
32 Farmers
33 Financial Resources
34 Technology Transfer
39 International Legal Instruments
40 Information.

Appendix 2
The Rio Declaration on Environment and Development

Preamble

The United Nations Conference on Environment and Development,
Having met at Rio de Janeiro from 3 to 14 June 1992,
Reaffirming the Declaration of the United Nations Conference on the Human Environment, adopted at Stockholm on 16 June 1972, and seeking to build upon it,
With the goal of establishing a new and equitable global partnership through the creation of new levels of cooperation among States, key sectors of societies and people,
Working towards international agreements which respect the interests of all and protect the integrity of the global environmental and developmental system,
Recognising the integral and interdependent nature of the Earth, our home,
Proclaims that:

Principle 1
Human beings are at the centre of concerns for sustainable development. They are entitled to a healthy and productive life in harmony with nature.

Principle 2
States have, in accordance with the Charter of the United Nations and the principles of international law, the sovereign right to exploit their own resources pursuant to their own environmental and developmental policies, and the responsibility to ensure that activities within their jurisdiction or control do not cause damage to the environment of other States or of areas beyond the limits of national jurisdiction.

Principle 3
The right to development must be fulfilled so as to equitably meet developmental and environmental needs of present and future generations.

Principle 4
In order to achieve sustainable development, environmental protection shall constitute an integral part of the development process and cannot be considered in isolation from it.

Principle 5
All States and all people shall cooperate in the essential task of eradicating poverty as an indispensable requirement for sustainable development, in order to decrease the disparities in standards of living and better meet the needs of the majority of the people of the world.

Principle 6
The special situation and needs of developing countries, particularly the least developed and those most environmentally vulnerable, shall be given special priority. International actions in the field of environment and development should also address the interests and needs of all countries.

Principle 7
States shall cooperate in a spirit of global partnership to conserve, protect and restore the health and integrity of the Earth's ecosystem. In view of the different contributions to global environmental degradation, States have common but differentiated responsibilities. The developed countries acknowledge the responsibility that they bear in the international pursuit of sustainable development in view of the pressures their societies place on the global environment and of the technologies and financial resources they command.

Principle 8
To achieve sustainable development and a higher quality of life for all people, States should reduce and eliminate unsustainable patterns of production and consumption and promote appropriate demographic policies.

Principle 9
States should cooperate to strengthen endogenous capacity-building for sustainable development by improving scientific understanding through exchanges of scientific and technological knowledge, and by enhancing the development, adaptation, diffusion and transfer of technologies, including new and innovative technologies.

Principle 10
Environmental issues are best handled with the participation of all concerned citizens, at the relevant level. At the national level, each individual shall have appropriate access to information concerning the environment that is held by public authorities, including information on hazardous materials and activities in their communities, and the opportunity to participate in decision-making processes. States shall facilitate and encourage public awareness and participation by making information widely available. Effective access to judicial and administrative proceedings, including redress and remedy, shall be provided.

Principle 11
States shall enact effective environmental legislation. Environmental standards, management objectives and priorities

should reflect the environmental and developmental context to which they apply. Standards applied by some countries may be inappropriate and of unwarranted economic and social cost to other countries, in particular developing countries.

Principle 12
States should cooperate to promote a supportive and open international economic system that would lead to economic growth and sustainable development in all countries, to better address the problems of environmental degradation. Trade policy measures for environmental purposes should not constitute a means of arbitrary or unjustifiable discrimination or a disguised restriction on international trade. Unilateral actions to deal with environmental challenges outside the jurisdiction of the importing country should be avoided. Environmental measures addressing transboundary or global environmental problems should, as far as possible, be based on an international consensus.

Principle 13
States shall develop national law regarding liability and compensation for the victims of pollution and other environmental damage. States shall also cooperate in an expeditious and more determined manner to develop further international law regarding liability and compensation for adverse effects of environmental damage caused by activities within their jurisdiction or control to areas beyond their jurisdiction.

Principle 14
States should effectively cooperate to discourage or prevent the relocation and transfer to other States of any activities and substances that cause severe environmental degradation or are found to be harmful to human health.

Principle 15
In order to protect the environment, the precautionary approach shall be widely applied by States according to their capabilities. Where there are threats of serious or irreversible damage, lack of full scientific certainty shall not be used as a reason for postponing cost-effective measures to prevent environmental degradation.

Principle 16
National authorities should endeavour to promote the internationalisation of environmental costs and the use of economic instruments, taking into account the approach that the polluter should, in

principle, bear the cost of pollution, with due regard to the public interest and without distorting international trade and investment.

Principle 17
Environmental impact assessment, as a national instrument, shall be undertaken for proposed activities that are likely to have a significant adverse impact on the environment and are subject to a decision of a competent national authority.

Principle 18
States shall immediately notify other States of any natural disasters or other emergencies that are likely to produce sudden harmful effects on the environment of those States. Every effort shall be made by the international community to help States so afflicted.

Principle 19
States shall provide prior and timely notification and relevant information to potentially affected States on activities that may have a significant adverse transboundary environmental effect and shall consult with those States at an early stage and in good faith.

Principle 20
Women have a vital role in environmental management and development. Their full participation is therefore essential to achieve sustainable development.

Principle 21
The creativity, ideals and courage of the youth of the world should be mobilised to forge a global partnership in order to achieve sustainable development and ensure a better future for all.

Principle 22
Indigenous people and their communities, and other local communities, have a vital role in environmental management and development because of their knowledge and traditional practices. States should recognise and duly support their identity, culture and interests and enable their effective participation in the achievement of sustainable development.

Principle 23
The environment and natural resources of people under oppression, domination and occupation shall be protected.

Principle 24
Warfare is inherently destructive of sustainable development. States shall therefore respect international law providing protection for the environment in times of armed conflict and cooperate in its further development, as necessary.

Principle 25
Peace, development and environmental protection are interdependent and indivisible.

Principle 26
States shall resolve all their environmental disputes peacefully and by appropriate means in accordance with the Charter of the United Nations.

Principle 27
States and people shall cooperate in good faith and in a spirit of partnership in the fulfilment of the principles embodied in this Declaration and in the further development of international law in the field of sustainable development.

Above: Architects of the Earth Summit: Gro Harlem Brundtland (centre) and Maurice Strong (right).

Appendix 3
Agenda 21 – Contents and Programme Areas

1 Preamble

Section I: Social and Economic Dimensions

2 International cooperation to accelerate sustainable development in developing countries and related domestic policies
A. Promoting sustainable development through trade
B. Making trade and environment mutually supportive
C. Providing adequate financial resources to developing countries
D. Encouraging economic policies conducive to sustainable development

3 Combating poverty – enabling the poor to achieve sustainable livelihoods; one programme area only with following activities:
– Empowering communities
– Management-related activities
– Data, information and evaluation
– International and regional cooperation and coordination

4 Changing consumption patterns
A. Focusing on unsustainable patterns of production and consumption
B. Developing national policies and strategies to encourage changes in unsustainable consumption patterns

5 Demographic dynamics and sustainability
A. Developing and disseminating knowledge concerning the links between demographic trends and factors and sustainable development
B. Formulating integrated national policies for environment and development, taking into account demographic trends and factors
C. Implementing integrated environment and development programmes at the local level, taking into account demographic trends and factors

6 Protection and promotion of human health
A. Meeting primary health care needs, particularly in rural areas
B. Control of communicable diseases
C. Protecting vulnerable groups
D. Meeting the urban health challenge
E. Reducing health risks from environmental pollution and hazards

7 Promoting sustainable human settlement development
A. Providing adequate shelter for all
B. Improving human settlement management
C. Promoting sustainable land use planning and management
D. Promoting the integrated provision of environmental infrastructure: water, sanitation, drainage and solid-waste management
E. Promoting sustainable energy and transport systems in human settlements
F. Promoting human settlement planning and management in disaster-prone areas
G. Promoting sustainable construction industry activities
H. Promoting human resource development and capacity-building for human settlements development

8 Integrating environment and development in decision-making
A. Integrating environment and development at the policy, planning and management levels
B. Providing an effective legal and regulatory framework
C. Making effective use of economic instruments and market and other incentives
D. Establishing systems for integrated environmental and economic accounting

Section II: Conservation and management of resources for development

9 Protection of the atmosphere
A. Addressing the uncertainties: improving the scientific basis for decision-making
B. Promoting sustainable development
C. Preventing stratospheric ozone depletion
D. Transboundary atmospheric pollution

10 Integrated approach to the planning and management of land resources; one programme area only with the following activities:
– Management-related activities
– Data and information
– International and regional coordination and cooperation

11 Combating deforestation
A. Sustaining the multiple roles and functions of all types of forests, forest lands and woodlands
B. Enhancing the protection, sustainable management and conservation of all forests, and the greening of degraded areas, through forest rehabilitation, afforestation, reforestation and other rehabilitative means
C. Promoting efficient utilisation and assessment to recover the full valuation of the goods and services provided by forests, forest lands and woodlands
D. Establishing and/or strengthening capacities for the planning, assessment and systematic observations of forests and related programmes, projects and activities, including commercial trade and processes

12 Managing fragile ecosystems: combating desertification and drought
A. Strengthening the knowledge base and developing information and monitoring systems for regions prone to desertification and drought, including the economic and social aspects of these ecosystems
B. Combating land degradation through, *inter alia*, intensified soil conservation, afforestation and reforestation activities
C. Developing and strengthening integrated development programmes for the eradication of poverty and promotion of alternative livelihood systems in areas prone to desertification
D. Developing comprehensive anti-desertification programmes and integrating them into national development plans and national environmental planning
E. Developing comprehensive drought preparedness and drought-relief schemes, including self-help arrangements, for drought-prone areas and designing programmes to cope with environmental refugees
F. Encouraging and promoting popular participation and environmental education, focusing on desertification control and management of the effects of drought

13 Managing fragile ecosystems: sustainable mountain development
A. Generating and strengthening knowledge about the ecology and sustainable development of mountain ecosystems
B. Promoting integrated watershed development and alternative livelihood opportunities

14 Promoting sustainable agriculture and rural development
A. Agricultural policy review, planning and integrated programmes in the light of the multifunctional aspect of agriculture, particularly with regard to food security and sustainable development
B. Ensuring people's participation and promoting human resource development for sustainable agriculture
C. Improving farm production and farming systems through diversification of farm and non-farm employment and infrastructure development
D. Land-resource planning, information and education for agriculture
E. Land conservation and rehabilitation
F. Water for sustainable food production and sustainable rural development
G. Conservation and sustainable utilisation of plant genetic resources for food and sustainable agriculture
H. Conservation and sustainable utilisation of animal genetic resources for sustainable agriculture

I. Integrated pest management and control in agriculture

J. Sustainable plant nutrition to increase food production

K. Rural energy transition to enhance productivity

L. Evaluation of the effects of ultraviolet radiation on plants and animals caused by the depletion of the stratospheric ozone layer

15 Conservation of biological diversity; one programme area only

16 Environmentally sound management of biotechnology

A. Increasing the availability of food, feed and renewable raw materials

B. Improving human health

C. Enhancing protection of the environment

D. Enhancing safety and developing international mechanisms for cooperation

E. Establishing enabling mechanisms for the development and the environmentally sound application of biotechnology

17 Protection of the oceans, all kinds of seas, including enclosed and semi-enclosed seas, and coastal areas and the protection, rational use and development of their living resources

A. Integrated management and sustainable development of coastal and marine areas, including exclusive economic zones

B. Marine environmental protection

C. Sustainable use and conservation of marine living resources of the high seas

D. Sustainable use and conservation of marine living resources under national jurisdiction

E. Addressing critical uncertainties for the management of the marine environment and climate change

F. Strengthening international, including regional, cooperation and coordination

G. Sustainable development of small islands

18 Protection of the quality and supply of freshwater resources: application of integrated approaches to the development, management and use of water resources

A. Integrated water resources development and management

B. Water resources assessment

C. Protection of water resources, water quality and aquatic ecosystems

D. Drinking-water supply and sanitation

E. Water and sustainable urban development

F. Water for sustainable food production and rural development

G. Impacts of climate change on water resources

19 Environmentally sound management of toxic chemicals, including prevention of illegal international traffic in toxic and dangerous products

A. Expanding and accelerating international assessment of chemical risks

B. Harmonisation of classification and labelling of chemicals

C. Information exchange on toxic chemicals and chemical risks

D. Establishment of risk reduction programmes

E. Strengthening of national capabilities and capacities for management of chemicals

F. Prevention of illegal international traffic in toxic and dangerous products

G. Enhancement of international cooperation relating to several of the programme areas

20 Environmentally sound management of hazardous wastes, including prevention of illegal international traffic in hazardous waste

A. Promoting the prevention and minimisation of hazardous waste

B. Promoting and strengthening institutional capacities in hazardous waste management

C. Promoting and strengthening international cooperation in the management of transboundary movements of hazardous wastes

D. Preventing illegal international traffic in hazardous wastes

21 Environmentally sound management of solid wastes and sewage-related issues

A. Minimising wastes

B. Maximising environmentally sound waste reuse and recycling

C. Promoting environmentally sound waste disposal and treatment

D. Extending waste service coverage

22 Safe and environmentally sound management of radioactive wastes; one programme area only with the following activities:

– Management-related activities

– International and regional cooperation and coordination

Section III: Strengthening the role of major groups

23 Preamble

24 Global action for women towards sustainable and equitable development; one programme area only

25 Children and youth in sustainable development

A. Advancing the role of youth and actively involving them in the protection of the environment and the promotion of economic and social development

B. Children in sustainable development

26 Recognising and strengthening the role of indigenous people and their communities; one programme area only

27 Strengthening the role of non-governmental organisations: partners for sustainable development; one programme area only

28 Local authorities' initiatives in support of *Agenda 21*; one programme area only

29 Strengthening the role of workers and their trade unions; one programme area only with the following activities:

– Promoting freedom of association

– Strengthening participation and consultation

– Providing adequate training

30 Strengthening the role of business and industry

A. Promoting cleaner production

B. Promoting responsible entrepreneurship

31 Scientific and technological community

A. Improving communication and cooperation among the scientific and technological community, decision makers and the public

B. Promoting codes of practice and guidelines related to science and technology

32 Strengthening the role of farmers; one programme area only

Section IV: Means of implementation

33 Financial resources and mechanisms

34 Transfer of environmentally sound technology: transfer, cooperation and capacity-building; one programme area only with the following activities:

– Development of international information networks which link national, subregional, regional and international systems

– Support and promotion of access to transfer of technology

– Improvement of the capacity to develop and manage environmentally sound technologies

– Establishment of a collaborative network of research centres

– Support for programmes of cooperation and assistance

– Technology assessment in support of the management of environmentally sound technology

– Collaborative arrangements and partnerships

35 Science for sustainable development

A. Strengthening the scientific basis for sustainable development

B. Enhancing scientific understanding

C. Improving long-term scientific assessment

D. Building up scientific capacity and capability

36 Promoting education, public awareness and training

A. Reorienting education towards

sustainable development
B. Increasing public awareness
C. Promoting training
37 National mechanisms and international cooperation for capacity-building; one programme area only with the following activities:
– Build a national consensus and formulate capacity-building strategies for implementing *Agenda 21*
– Identify national sources and present of requests for technical cooperation, including that related to technology transfer and know-how in the

framework of sector strategies
– Establish of a review mechanism of technical cooperation in and related to technology transfer and know-how
– Enhance the expertise and collective contribution of the United Nations system for capacity and capability-building initiatives
– Harmonise the delivery of assistance at the regional level
38 International institutional arrangements; one programme area only
39 International legal instruments and

mechanisms; one programme area only with the following activities:
– Review, assessment and fields of action in international law for sustainable development
– Implementation mechanisms
– Effective participation in international law-making
– Disputes in the field of sustainable development
40 Information for decision-making
A. Bridging the data gap
B. Improving information availability

General Assembly Debates UNCED follow-up

In late autumn 1992, the agreements made at the Rio Earth Summit were presented to the 47th United Nations General Assembly session for formal endorsement. The Rio recommendations concerning the UN Commission on Sustainable Development were central to the debate.

There were few if any surprises during the General Assembly debate. Sufficient support was obtained from the Rio recommendations to allow optimistic observers to proclaim that the outcome was positive, while enough key areas were left vague or ill-defined to allow the pessimists to assert that it was too early to judge.

Some of the principal recommendations contained in the resolution on "Institutional arrangements to follow-up UNCED" are as follows:

■ Endorsement for the recommendations on international institutional arrangements contained in *Agenda 21*. These have been described in Chapter 8 of *Facing the Future*;
■ It is recommended that the Commission on Sustainable Development (CSD) should:
– have the broad function to monitor both progress in the implementation of *Agenda 21* and the integration of environment and development within the UN system. Specifically the CSD should give consideration to reports from governments concerning difficulties faced in implementing *Agenda 21*, with a focus on constraints such as finance and technology transfer;
– review and monitor progress towards the UN target of 0.7 per cent of GNP for aid, and link progress with Agenda 21 implementation with the finances available. In other words, no money, no progress;
– consider input from NGOs, and enhance the participation of, and dialogue with, these groups and the independent sector. This could serve to catalyse what some have called the "international civil society";
– promote the incorporation of the Rio Declaration and the Forest Principles in the implementation of *Agenda 21*;
– recognise that the implementation of *Agenda 21* is a dynamic programme subject to review and evolution;

■ The CSD will consist of 53 States elected by ECOSOC, and will strive to be more representative of both developing and developed country opinion by paying due regard to "equitable geographical distribution". The regional allocation of seats will be the same as in the Commission on Science and Technology for Development. This addresses developing country concerns for fair access to international decision making;
■ The Secretary General has been asked to submit his proposals for the rules of procedure for the CSD, to the next organisational session of ECOSOC, taking into account existing procedures, and commitments to the participation of NGOs;
■ The CSD should organise its work along a "multi-thematic" programme of work to ensure an integrated and cross-sectoral treatment of *Agenda 21* implementation;
■ The CSD should also organise its work in three segments:
– Finance, transfer of technology, capacity building, and other cross-sectoral issues;
– Review of *Agenda 21* implementation at the international, regional, and national level;
– A high-level meeting with ministerial participation.

Such organisation is designed to make the work programme manageable, although what it will mean in practice is unclear.

■ At the first substantive session of the CSD, the Secretary General should provide a review of progress in implementation of *Agenda 21*, containing information on finance, technology transfer, the UN system, assistance to the national reports process, and major and emerging issues;
■ All specialised UN agencies and related organisations of the UN system are asked to strengthen and adjust their activities to be in line with *Agenda 21*. UNEP and UNDP will present their action plans to the next General Assembly meeting, through the CSD and through ECOSOC. How far this will result in a repackaging of existing activities rather than a radical revision is too early to judge;
■ The World Bank and other financial agencies are requested to submit regular reports to the CSD on their experience with *Agenda 21* implementation. This amounts to a rather

weak oversight role for the CSD, which still leaves the World Bank "on the outside";
■ The General Assembly endorsed the idea of a High-Level Advisory Board to the Secretary General, and through him/her to the Commission, ECOSOC and the General Assembly. This Board should consist of expert eminent persons, recognised in their field, with a very broad brief to advise on issues related to the implementation of *Agenda 21*;
■ A request has been made to the Secretary General to set up a CSD Secretariat as a "clearly identifiable entity", which is gender and geographically balanced, to support the Commission, the Inter-Agency Commission on Sustainable Development, and the High-Level Advisory Board.

Inevitably, great uncertainties exist as to whether the Commission on Sustainable Development will have any clout. For example, some observers believe that the institutions resolution does not bring the World Bank and the Bretton Woods institutions sufficiently within a framework of international accountability. This raises the spectre of a "parallel UN" made up of the World Bank, the IMF and the GATT. Other observers such as GreenPeace have similar concerns that transnational corporations are not accountable to any UN body.

It is still unclear where exactly the Secretariat is to be placed within the UN hierarchy. Will it be close enough to UN power structures or independent enough to work effectively? Much also depends upon who is appointed to head the Secretariat.

The Commission on Sustainable Development will not be the tough uncompromising watchdog advocated by some NGOs. Its present mandate lacks a role in resolving environmental conflicts or investigating violations of the Earth Summit and other international environment and development agreements. In spirit, the Commission will serve an "enabling", constructive role, rather than acting as a global policeman.

This effectively leaves the independent watchdog and "whistle-blowing" role to the NGOs. Some would question, therefore, whether the UN has made any genuine political commitment to openness, freedom of information, and accountability.